D0687887

CULTURE SHOCK

An unstoppable force is changing how we work and live. Gallup's solution to the biggest leadership issue of our time.

Jim Clifton | Jim Harter

GALLUP PRESS
The Gallup Building
901 F Street, NW
Washington, D.C. 20004

Library of Congress Control Number: 2022951903
ISBN: 978-1-59562-247-1

First Printing: 2023
10 9 8 7 6 5 4 3 2 1

Printed in Canada by Friesens

Table of Contents

Part 1: What Work and Life Do People Want?

Chapter 1: The Awakening 3

Chapter 2: The New Freedom 9

Chapter 3: The Business Problem 13

Chapter 4: The Role Human Nature Plays in Business
    Outcomes 17

Chapter 5: The Most Important Habit of a Great Manager 29

Part 2: Future Culture

Chapter 6: The Shift 35

Chapter 7: Why the Commute? 39

Chapter 8: Is In-Person Time That Valuable? 43

Chapter 9: The Right Mix 47

Chapter 10: Splitters and Blenders: Two Different
    Relationships to Work 51

Chapter 11: The Other Half — On-site Workers 55

Chapter 12: Is the Four-Day Workweek a Good Idea? 59

Chapter 13: The Reshuffling 65

Chapter 14: In Decline: Employee Engagement 71

Chapter 15: The Risk of Not Caring About Employee
    Wellbeing 77

Chapter 16: Increasing Employee-Employer Disconnect 81

Chapter 17: How to Win in the New Environment 85

Part 3: Strengths to Role

Chapter 18: How Do We Know if Employees Are Productive?..... 91

Chapter 19: Systems That Work Against Human Nature 97

Chapter 20: Strengths Pioneer — Peter Drucker............................. 103

Chapter 21: Strengths Pioneer — Abraham Maslow...................... 107

Chapter 22: Strengths Pioneer — Don Clifton 111

Chapter 23: Fitting Strengths to Role at the Highest
Leadership Levels.. 117

Chapter 24: Coaching Strengths to Role at the Highest
Leadership Levels.. 121

Chapter 25: Why Build a Strengths-Based Culture? 125

Chapter 26: Steps to Building a Strengths-Based Culture.......... 129

Part 4: 70% Manager

Chapter 27: The Manager Breakthrough 137

Chapter 28: One Meaningful Conversation With Each
Employee per Week... 141

Chapter 29: How to Make Meaningful Conversations a
Weekly Habit 145

Chapter 30: The Hard Job of Managing 149

Part 5: Gallup's CEO Playbook

Our Recommendations for the New Workplace............................. 155

Appendix: Gallup Meta-Analyses of Gallup Path Linkages..... 161

References **265**

About Gallup..**289**

About the Authors **291**

Acknowledgments **293**

PART 1

What Work and Life Do People Want?

CHAPTER 1
The Awakening

Who knew that the whole world could switch their office jobs to home jobs overnight?

Who knew that millions of daily commutes could stop and the business world would still work?

Who knew that business travel could become permanently unnecessary overnight?

An awakening shocked the world — a structural change in how humans work and live. We wrote this book for our clients, thought leaders and friends in high places. Nothing is going back to normal. This is a moment of evolutionary change.

How we adapt to this culture shock — the *new will of the world* — will determine whether U.S. and global productivity will go up or down.

Gallup's solution outlines a better world of work and life — one with far higher productivity and higher wellbeing — both of which needed to be fixed anyway.

The coming danger

The danger is that a majority of employees will now operate more like independent contractors or gig workers than employees who are loyal and committed to your organization. The risk grows as your workforce's mindset continues to shift from "my life at work" to "my life at home," making it nearly impossible to create a culture of committed team members and powerful relationships at work.

A big question leaders have been asking is: *How do we bring employees back?* The greater issue is deteriorating customer relationships, which is already happening. The most serious financial issue is customer retention, not employee retention. The American Customer Satisfaction Index reported declines in customer satisfaction with U.S. companies starting in 2019, with steep drops in 2020 through 2022. Employees are also now less likely to say that their organization delivers on its promise to customers.

Simply put, your employees and customers know each other. Many are best friends. All the good stuff in human nature and behavioral economics between employees and customers is at risk. How will you maintain your customers' commitment if you're struggling to create a culture of dedicated employees who build and strengthen relationships with those customers?

Many executives have wondered if office workers, administrators and managers are secretly trying to go part time and still be paid full time.

Unless we go through a massive workplace transformation, the new will of the world will leave your organization unimaginably less engaged, because people have now experienced a new way to work that serves their *lives* better. But the real fallout isn't here yet. The real fallout will come when the storm of declining employee engagement hits the customer.

As of this writing, Gallup's deepest and most comprehensive data on the post-COVID-19 workplace are from the U.S., and U.S. employee engagement has reached a seven-year low.

Here is what American employees told us: 56% of 125 million full-time workers said they don't have to be in the workplace anymore because they discovered, thanks to a pandemic, that they can now do their job from home — or lakeside or suburban acreage.

According to Gallup, a staggering 90% of U.S. employees with desk and office jobs aren't longing for the old workplace to return. Only CEOs are. Many employees have refused to go back. It is no longer a privilege to work in a cool shiny steel building with enchanting water sounds in the lobby.

In fact, Gallup researchers find that if a building in downtown Chicago, Dallas or Los Angeles had 500 people in it before the pandemic, it now has about 300 people in it. Many thought leaders believed the numbers would go back closer to the old normal — as much as 90% of employees on-site. We predict that number will soon be 50%+ *at best* on any given day compared with the same day in 2019.

COVID-19 made us sick, killed millions worldwide, crushed families, stunted learning for kids, and disrupted how we work and live — not to mention, it destroyed one-third of small businesses. COVID-19 remains a historic human catastrophe. Much of the devastation is still coming as the massive stimulus from Washington winds down.

But the pandemic also made extraordinary societal and economic progress possible.

The new will of the workplace

Employees and executives have now experienced a world we couldn't have dreamed of before — a new, seemingly magical, all-virtual workplace where every day of the week is a work-life blend.

Are you open to the possibility that we are suddenly more productive than we have been in 50 years — but work just looks different?

The authors of this book feel we are more productive in many ways ourselves just because our continuous travel stopped. We now do hundreds of Zoom meetings and very little travel. So we can put in more hours of high-concentration work. For decades, we were on the road most weeks — and 25% minimum was transit time. You could argue we had been part time ourselves, and the pandemic moved us to full time. The total number and frequency of our team and customer meetings is way up. So that's good. As to effectiveness — yet to be learned.

Proud road warriors can see multiples more customers per week now via Zoom. Road warriors face extinction. Airlines and hotels will have far fewer business travelers. They will need to reset for mostly tourism and personal travel.

A very slow-moving train carrying an all-digital workplace that we thought would arrive about 2040 is here now.

Can you imagine having a pre-pandemic business lunch and a visitor from the future joins and reports, "Oh yeah, there is a monster pandemic coming that will crush humankind. And get this, everybody will permanently work at home so we don't need cities and towering office buildings anymore, nor all the supporting retail. Airlines and hotels will lose their high-margin business travelers. Dramatic declines in business lunches and dinners will create half-empty cafes, and a third of them will go broke."

We are all in the most serious survival test of the last 50 years — a real trial of life. We need to make unthinkable changes. We must grow — so goes business growth, so go shareholders, families and jobs, taxes for schools, healthcare, fire and police, and infrastructure — and so on.

The solution starts with addressing the new *will of the workplace*.

Gallup finds that we have been very slowly drifting to hybrid work — a blend of working on-site and from home — for years. Fridays were already gone. And staying home to do a project on Mondays was becoming easy to do without asking for permission. CEOs were not concerned about the declining office occupancy because just like global warming and the national debt, the potential disaster was a long way away — so they went back to work and didn't worry about it.

Who knew that everyone in the whole world with an office or desk job could check into "Hotel Zoom International" at the same time. A spectacular digital advancement for humankind came wrapped inside a global health catastrophe.

Work and life have been hit by an asteroid — one that will change America and the world differently than the Great Recession and as much or more than the Great Depression — because this time, there isn't a return to anything resembling normal.

This culture shock is more like when Americans moved from farms to factories in the early 1900s. Cities boomed. Up to 40% of the U.S. workforce was employed by farms early in the last century. Today, just a little over 1% work on farms.

U.S. workers now want work to fit into life versus forcing life to fit into work. More like France. The French tend to define their lives as their time away from work. Americans historically have defined their lives by their time at work.

Because of a global pandemic, citizens and families discovered a new future of work and life — a work life that doesn't require cars, trains, planes or buses. A work life that offers time away from stress created by lousy managers, which might be the biggest benefit of all. Employees at all levels, including the executive committee, found a new freedom, and they love it.

CHAPTER 2
The New Freedom

"Morning boss, it's Rajesh. I am Zooming in from my new lake home. Great news. I moved to South Carolina. So cool — my boat house is my office!"

Boss: "WTF? You must be kidding. Are you going part time? Are you retiring? You are only 40 years old!"

CEOs are all getting these calls. Rajesh didn't move to a lake house to wait out COVID-19. He has moved there permanently. He changed how he lives. He changed his relationship to his work and life.

Gallup finds that 50% of U.S. employees now want their work and life blended.

But it's important to know that most remote-ready employees *always* wanted work and life blended, yet nobody knew it was this easy. Blending work and life is now inextricably woven into the Great American Dream and Great Global Dream. Your new hires are already demanding the freedom to choose when and if they come in each day. They don't want a more liberal policy on "required days in office." They want no policy at all — including your hardest working stars.

Your instincts as a leader are to fight the will. "Come back to work or you are fired."

A very talented analyst candidate told us, "I would love to join Gallup. It has been a dream of mine to work here. My one and only requirement is that there is no requirement for days in the office." He wasn't looking for a policy of two or three days per week. He was looking for a policy of *total freedom to choose*. There it is. He is a very hard worker, but he requires the new freedom.

If you are waiting for "normal" to return, are you sure that's what you want?

Are you open to the fact that we need to reinvent how we develop people because the old way stopped working years ago? Why do so many people not want to be at your workplace? Or did they ever? Why have so many chosen to be gig-like?

50% of U.S. employees now want their **work and life blended**.

Gallup's breakthrough is that the new will of the worker is to work mostly from home because: #1) no more commuting, #2) higher wellbeing and #3) works better for their family.

The pandemic exposed a blind spot in leaders' view of work: Employees absolutely abhor daily commuting — and not just lower-level workers. The CEO and the executive committee despise it too but have always had total freedom to choose when they come in and jobs that don't confine them to a desk for decades.

Over the years, Gallup missed asking *why* people who have desk jobs are required to travel miles from their home to sit in what is basically just a different chair. Like many things, we just assumed there was no better way.

As Daniel Kahneman said, "Our comforting conviction that the world makes sense rests on a secure foundation: our almost unlimited ability to ignore our ignorance."

The new freedom is that every morning, you get to choose whether you go in. And it works for now, because your customers and your team members are doing the same thing. You don't need to be in the office for the day's assignments, and neither do they.

Again, how this affects productivity will depend on how we react. It will depend on developing a new global theory of work. Ask yourself: Are you more or less productive in the new hybrid workplace?

We predict that many people will eventually experience higher wellbeing and declining burnout — but followed by significantly lower productivity because teams won't function as effectively, and customer relationships will deteriorate.

CHAPTER 3
The Business Problem

You probably haven't heard this: "Our employees and front-line managers control customer outcomes and daily cash flow more than any other single lever we can pull."

Your employees have customers who are their best friends at work. In every company in the world, a certain percentage of employees talk to customers every day. They live customer centricity, which is now likely in serious decline, according to Gallup data.

The business media doesn't know this either. They only see the pandemic causing an *employee* crisis. However, Gallup predicts that the real impact will come from a *customer* crisis.

Fast declining employee engagement puts your customer retention at risk. Your employees are the closest thing to your customers, and customers are the closest thing to cash.

When you lose an engaged employee, it impacts your customers and to some degree, changes your company's stock price. Every positive or negative employee-customer interaction moves your stock price up or down a little.

This is why human nature has such a powerful influence on hard business outcomes. But board members don't pay attention to this stuff because they can't see the connection.

Board members don't really care about employee engagement because they can't see its connection to day-to-day business outcomes — such as the week's cash flow.

Some CEOs feign caring by reporting the "S" in their ESG (Environmental, Social and Governance) standards through promoting their employee engagement scores. In publicly held board meetings all around the world, the CHRO enters for 30 minutes to give the HR report. And they always say, "Our engagement is 80%." And then people clap, and the CHRO leaves with the board believing 80% of their employees are engaged.

These CHROs measure "engagement" using a satisfaction scale of 1-5 and calculate the percentage of engaged employees by adding the 4s and 5s together. The problem is, 4s aren't 5s when it comes to predicting customer retention.

If you do simple analytics with more demanding question items and business outcomes, you will find that in U.S. companies, only about 30% of employees are truly engaged. Another 20% are miserable and spreading their misery in the workplace, and 50% are just showing up — wishing they didn't have to work at all — especially in this job.

What if your organization reported only 5s in response to this item: *There is someone at work who encourages my development.* A 5 rating creates more cash flow and more customer buildout — and all the other good things. A 5 does — a 4 does not. A 4 means your employees are not sure. If they were, they would say 5.

For example, when all employees on a team respond with a 5 (strongly agree) to employee engagement items, they have 28% lower turnover rates than average. Those who respond with a 4 have only 4% better than average turnover rates. Improvement in customer loyalty is negligible for employees on teams that give a 4 rating.

14

Why Gallup Focuses on 5s

Moving the needle on business outcomes

Outcome	Strongly disagree 1	2	3	4	Strongly agree 5
Productivity	-31%	-20%	-9%	2%	13%
Turnover	67%	43%	19%	-4%	-28%
Customer loyalty	-17%	-11%	-5%	1%	7%
Safety (accidents)	97%	62%	28%	-7%	-42%

Average utility across Gallup overall satisfaction and Q^{12} items
Difference from average for each scale point
Gallup Q^{12} meta-analysis database including 82,248 business units across 230 organizations
Source: Gallup

Life is about having great customers

In the U.S., 70% of total GDP is retail sales. When shoppers hit the checkout lines with 10% less in their shopping carts, the whole country's GDP tanks. The whole world's GDP tanks when customers and employees buy and sell less.

Businesses aren't the only ones with customers. Museums have customers, nonprofits have customers, doctors and hospitals have customers, K-12 schools have customers (kids and parents), mayors have customers (citizens), universities have customers (few know it), foundations have customers, and some of us have internal customers.

A good question to ask is: *How many customers can you create?* Period. That is the very origin of rising economic energy in your organization. In the absence of great customers, there are no fulfilled missions, no booming stock increases, no increasing numbers of great jobs, no great companies and no great societies.

CHAPTER 4
The Role Human Nature Plays in Business Outcomes

Many executives and thought leaders ask Gallup, "Can you please tell us, as specifically as possible, the role human nature, feelings and relationships play in creating customers and driving business outcomes?"

We did that. It's called The Gallup Path — a quarter century of global meta-analytics conclusions on one page, in one picture. It is our simplest illustration of how behavioral economics — feelings and emotions — drive revenue growth, earnings and stock price.

Before we go through The Gallup Path, you must believe that your sales go up or down to some degree based on every single human interaction.

This is Gallup's conclusion from the biggest workplace study — ever. Here's what we found: The best predictor of stock increase is earnings increase. Period. So we will start there.

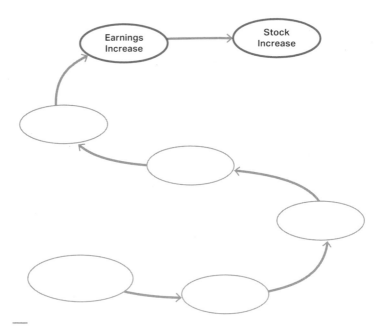

Earnings Increase

Stock Increase

The Gallup Path®

The role human nature plays in business outcomes

There are other factors that increase stock price, such as acquisitions, stock buybacks, a leadership change the media likes and new product announcements. But the one that best correlates year over year and decade over decade is simply *earnings increase*. Increased/decreased earnings explain almost all the variation in stock prices, controlling for market fluctuations.

The surest way to increase earnings is to cut costs. CEOs and executive committees work on that most of the time — reducing costs or driving down supplier prices and payroll. Management consultants are primarily cost cutters. These are all good things and what most CEOs are best at.

Cost cutting works, but after a while, it hits a wall. At some point, companies have to expand their customer base. These are two separate leadership activities — and both are absolute requirements of running any organization well.

Let's call cost cutting the defense and creating customers the offense. The Gallup Path drives the offense.

What most predictably drives earnings increase? *Revenue growth.*

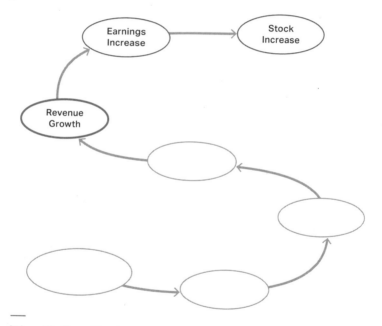

The Gallup Path®

The role human nature plays in business outcomes

Revenue growth begins with keeping the customers you have. Customer retention is the most critical metric on a CEO's dashboard. Building out customers is the second most important.

And third is acquiring new customers — where leaders spend most of their time, even as their best customers trickle away. As we noted earlier, customer satisfaction is tanking. Losing customers is the new biggest risk created by the culture shock.

The best *earned* cash flow comes from keeping and nurturing the customers you have. CEOs know this, but it seems hard for them to remember.

Let's keep going.

Revenue growth is the best predictor of real *earnings increase*. These three bubbles are what you learn to use in MBA classes and consulting training. They are the classic business economics of the last 100 years.

So, what predictably moves revenue growth across all industries?

Customer engagement — a *feeling* from your customers that you are an essential partner who adds value to their business or life and who cares about their success. That is behavioral economics — where *feelings become facts*.

When your customers feel that you add value and care about their success, they buy more, transact more frequently, are less price sensitive and are more likely to recommend. Engaged customers are typically 25% of your customer base.

The next question is: What is the primary driver of customer engagement? Our scientists dove deep into our world's largest data pool — with meta-analytics across more than 100,000 business units to find out.

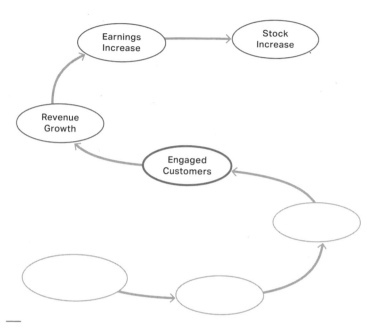

The Gallup Path®

The role human nature plays in business outcomes

Engaged customers create your growth, earnings and stock price — your *engaged employees* create your engaged customers.

When your employees and teams are inspired, love their jobs, and believe in the mission and purpose of their organization, you retain and grow customers and beat your competitors.

When your employees hate their organization and their boss, the client feels it.

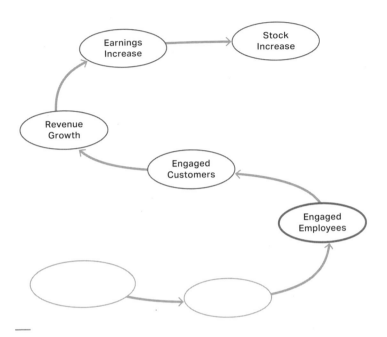

The Gallup Path®

The role human nature plays in business outcomes

Customer-employee interactions move the sales needle, up or down, more than any other single factor in every organization in the world. This is where declining employee engagement crushes customer centricity — and subsequently revenue growth, earnings and stock price.

Here is a bit of customer survey engineering: On a scale of 1-5 with 5 being high (strongly agree), the single most important futuristic metric is *percentage of 5s* on customer engagement — 5s predict success, 4s don't. Percentage of 5s on customer engagement is the best way for a CEO to evaluate overall future corporate performance.

When an organization improves its number of 5 ratings from 25% to 35%, sales rise, profit increases and stock prices go up. If there is a silver bullet for leading revenue growth, it is dramatically boosting this customer score.

This is why a winning culture for any type of organization is one of relentless customer focus.

Several years ago at a Business Round Table event in Colorado Springs, Jeff Bezos approached one of us with his hand extended. Rather than introduce himself or say, "Hi Jim," he said, "Have you tried Prime?" He didn't want to know how Jim thought the conference was going. He didn't want to know about Gallup. He wanted to know if Jim and the other people standing around had tried his new product, Prime. How customer intense is this guy?

Imagine *that* heightened level of customer intensity in all companies. '

Increasing employee engagement shoots human energy through the other four bubbles on The Gallup Path, and like magic, you have revenue growth, increased earnings and finally — increased stock price.

So how do you increase employee engagement? A crucial breakthrough in this book is this: Fitting *strengths to role* is essential to winning in business, science, education, sports or anything. If you stumble here, nothing else matters.

Peter Drucker said, "Few people, even highly successful people, can answer the questions: Do you know what you're good at? Do you know what you need to learn so that you get the full benefit of your strengths?"

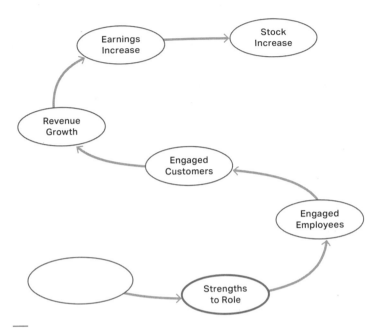

The Gallup Path®

The role human nature plays in business outcomes

Drucker also said, "The task of leadership is to create an alignment of strengths in ways that make weaknesses irrelevant."

Some managers and coaches have natural instincts to "fit" someone's strengths to their role; others can learn and greatly improve at it. Any manager can learn how to fit strengths to role as a competency.

Gallup's biggest global workplace discovery is that a staggering 70% of the variance in team engagement is determined by *just the manager.* So go your managers, so go employee engagement, customer 5s, revenue growth, earnings and eventually, your stock price.

Almost no CEO, board member or investor knows that. The quality of the manager is the lowest hanging fruit for soaring customer success and real revenue growth and earnings increase. The most predictable lever in your entire organization to drive the power of behavioral economics is the manager.

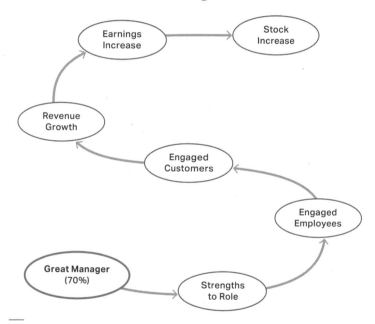

The Gallup Path®

The role human nature plays in business outcomes

What did Gallup find that clearly differentiates a great manager from an average one? The shortest answer is that they are experts at putting people in roles that use their natural strengths. The other thing they do differently is *coach* versus administrate (think forms and spreadsheets). Administrating teams is important and necessary, but every person in every role needs a masterful coach.

There it is.

The Gallup Path is our best illustration of the behavioral economic linkages from the manager all the way to stock increase. Something very similar to this has been referred to as the "service profit chain." Our data confirm and significantly expand on these linkages scientifically across thousands of business units.

CHAPTER 5
The Most Important Habit of a Great Manager

According to Gallup's workplace science, the *manager* is the very origin of new economic energy. If you can remember that finding, it will change all your economic outcomes.

It will be crucial for future managers to create opportunities for each employee to use their strengths and minimize their weaknesses. Great managers know their employees' strengths and give them a role they can grow in with no limits. Getting this wrong is the root cause of burnout. Giving a person a task they have little capacity to perform grinds the life out of them and leads to mental health issues.

Unfortunately, nearly one in five U.S. workers rate their mental health as fair or poor. These workers report about 4x more unplanned absences due to mental health than their counterparts who report good, very good or excellent mental health.

When our chief scientist was asked to define as specifically as possible the *most important* habit of a great manager, his answer was: *One meaningful conversation per week with each team member.*

The question that always follows is, "What is a meaningful conversation?" The answer is, "Focusing on the employee's goals." Discussing goals leads to customer retention, team collaboration, recognition and wellbeing.

To win in the new hybrid workplace, you need to adjust your culture dashboard so it includes asking your employees to respond — on the same 1-5 scale we used earlier — to this statement:

I have received meaningful feedback in the past week.

This is the ultimate measure of the effectiveness of your managers because it is about weekly, not annual, feedback. It is the right metric, the right habit, for true coaching effectiveness in the hybrid workplace.

Only 5s matter on this one too. You are probably running at 20% to 30% 5s. When you move that metric to 50%, you have not only solved customer retention, but you have also successfully completed the two primary demands of the hybrid global workplace: fitting strengths to role and having the right conversations.

A new dashboard

A quarter century ago, after testing hundreds of workplace question items, Gallup found that if we knew how any employee at any level answered 12 highly tested items, we knew how they would answer virtually anything else we could ask them. These items are known as the Q^{12}, and thousands of big, medium and small organizations around the world use them.

The Gallup Q¹²

Q01. I know what is expected of me at work.

Q02. I have the materials and equipment I need to do my work right.

Q03. At work, I have the opportunity to do what I do best every day.

Q04. In the last seven days, I have received recognition or praise for doing good work.

Q05. My supervisor, or someone at work, seems to care about me as a person.

Q06. There is someone at work who encourages my development.

Q07. At work, my opinions seem to count.

Q08. The mission or purpose of my company makes me feel my job is important.

Q09. My associates or fellow employees are committed to doing quality work.

Q10. I have a best friend at work.

Q11. In the last six months, someone at work has talked to me about my progress.

Q12. This last year, I have had opportunities at work to learn and grow.

Since the pandemic, Gallup researchers have added four items to address *Respect* (diversity, equity and inclusion), *Wellbeing* (burnout/mental health), *Coaching habit* (one conversation per week) and *Customer* (promises).

Gallup has created a reengineered dashboard for the new hybrid world. We call it Q^{12+} — now 16 items plus your highly individualized, client-specific questions.

PART 2
Future Culture

CHAPTER 6
The Shift

In the spring of 2020, the percentage of U.S. employees working from home some of the time more than doubled, from 25% pre-COVID-19 to 65% in late April and early May.

Some employees' jobs were already set up for working from home. Others were configured to work from remote environments part of the time. And still others had to transition quickly from 0% to 100% remote. Before the pandemic, only 6% of the U.S. workforce worked from home full time.

COVID-19 surges brought with them starts and stops in returning to the office. Organizations' plans ranged from ordering people back to the office to nudging them and from offering incentives to giving up altogether on people ever coming back.

Yet in 2022, four out of every 10 employees worked from home at least some of the time. Among those with remote-ready jobs, nearly eight out of 10 employees worked from home full time or at least some of the time.

Based on surveys of the new remote work experience, in the spring of 2020, Gallup predicted that COVID-19 would create the "next normal" workplace.

Since the pandemic began, Gallup has continuously asked workers about their experiences and preferences. We found that nearly seven in 10 full-time employees in the U.S. prefer some type of remote work arrangement. That compares with four in 10 who already have one. Among those with remote-ready jobs, *nine in 10* want some type of remote work arrangement.

Gallup found that a preference for fully remote work is driven primarily by five factors: commute time, wellbeing, flexibility for family, productivity and fewer distractions.

Employees who prefer on-site work said they find it more productive and easier to collaborate. They also said they have better access to technology and feel more connected to the organization — and it improves their wellbeing.

It took a pandemic-induced experiment to learn how people really want to work. What we discovered shouldn't have come as a surprise, but it did. Prior to the pandemic, the perk employees wanted most was flextime. More than half of workers told Gallup they would change employers for a flexible schedule.

Scientific literature suggests that when employees have the freedom to choose when and how they do their work, creativity and innovation increase. This concept is called "task autonomy." Nearly 40% of employees tell Gallup they would change jobs for the option to work full or part time from a flexible location. This figure hasn't changed since 2016.

The desire for autonomy is not new, but the freedom is. Having *experienced* it, freedom has become irrevocable for employees.

The "endowment effect" — a behavioral economic term for the emotional bias that causes you to value something more highly once you own it than you did before you owned it — applies here. Experiments have found that the financial value someone places on a simple coffee mug doubles once they possess and then sell it.

And a newfound workplace freedom is a lot bigger deal than a coffee mug.

CHAPTER 7
Why the Commute?

Working in the same place we sleep is deeply embedded in our brains. Maybe that's why working from home felt so familiar once the pandemic hit.

Throughout history, working from home has been the norm. Hunter-gatherers in primitive societies worked in their homes preparing food and making clothes.

Working from home was not just a primitive way of life. It was also common in the Middle Ages. For example, working-class people in England plied their trades and crafts from home — their work and life were combined. A more recent variation of this is British couples who own pubs and serve pints of beer during the day or evening and live in a flat upstairs.

The Industrial Revolution brought with it skilled factory work that required people to travel to a plant or mill and work on-site. Yet throughout the 19th century and some of the 20th, many people continued to work from home — providing services like laundry and food for factory workers.

The modern-day office didn't emerge until the 20th century, driven by advances in technology — electricity, telephones, public transportation. Eventually, the once-normal practice of working from home — coined "telecommuting" in the 1970s — became the exception. In 2019, less than 5% of people in the U.S. worked full time from home.

Commuting to work eventually became part of our work culture. The expectation to show up in person, looking our best, became the standard. Being in the office influenced how others perceived us. We could have a big impact simply through our physical proximity to our colleagues and bosses.

In 2019, **less than 5% of people** in the U.S. worked full time from home.

Commuting became further embedded in our work culture because of a depressing aspect of human nature — the concept of "learned helplessness," which results from people accepting a norm because they think they can't change it.

Also, like many other animals, humans have a herd instinct. There is safety in numbers. We're social creatures who generally like to be with other people and often get more done in teams.

Deep in our brains, traveling to be together is natural. We do it for worship, sporting events, concerts, dinner parties and the like. And we've done it for work since the Industrial Revolution.

Does commuting still make sense?

Next time you fly over a large city in the morning or evening, notice the endless line of slow-moving cars for as far as you can see. And consider that the people in those cars are not living their best lives during those hours on the road. When you look at it this way, commuting seems like one of humankind's worst ideas.

We created entertainment and fast food to make the commute more tolerable. We invented an industry of morning and late afternoon radio talk shows, audiobooks and podcasts.

But commuting has become more and more stressful. In 2019, the U.S. Census Bureau reported that the average one-way commute to work was 27.6 minutes; this is an increase of 10% from 2006. That's 230 hours a year to and from work — the equivalent of almost 29 eight-hour workdays.

Employers typically don't include the time employees spend in traffic or on trains in a 40-hour workweek. So increased commute times have crowded out leisure time. And research has found that people's satisfaction with their leisure time declines significantly as their commute time increases.

Long commutes are also associated with high blood pressure, tension, anger, stiff necks, fatigue, lower back pain and obesity. Gallup has found that commutes of 45 minutes or more are linked to poorer overall wellbeing, daily mood and health. And in 2022, Gallup found that commutes of just 30 minutes are linked to higher stress and anger. After being able to avoid commuting during the pandemic, even half an hour now feels intolerable for many people.

Knocking out the commute produced an awakening in a world of office workers who concluded, "Work doesn't have to be done this way."

CHAPTER 8
Is In-Person Time That Valuable?

Whether they're commuting or not, people still rely on social bonds to get work done. Mandated social distancing and a shift to Zoom didn't change that one bit. In fact, Gallup meta-analysis of over 100,000 business units found that teams with more coworkers who were bonded achieve higher performance and lower turnover.

There are deep-seated reasons for this. Anthropologists contend that human brain size grew over time to enable greater computational power. We needed this power to keep up with our various social interconnections and to expand our number of meaningful connections. Social bonds offered humans protection from predators and greater capacity for collaborating, trading for food and resources, and hunting larger game.

Throughout most of history, our social interactions have been in person. The digital world of the past few decades is new to our brains. To what extent can we replicate a satisfying and bonding social experience through technology?

Years before the pandemic, Gallup conducted an in-depth study of social time use and its impact on daily mood. We asked 17,719 panel members to reconstruct their previous day. For each part of the day — morning, afternoon and evening — we asked them to tell us how much time they spent socializing, what kind of social time it was and how they felt.

Gallup found that nearly all forms of social time boosted mood, but after about 25% of the day spent socializing via technology, people's moods dropped. In-person social time had the largest positive impact on mood — *but the total amount of time mattered less than the event itself.* Exercising or eating/drinking together had the strongest impact on mood. Compared with in-person time, videoconferencing had a weaker effect on mood.

Among hybrid employees, 32% indicate that virtual meetings are less effective than in-person meetings, compared with 17% who say virtual meetings are more effective. More than half (51%) say there is no difference.

Yet there are advantages to being in the same place as colleagues. As we mention above, Gallup's study of social time shows that being with other people results in better moods. We build trust more quickly in person. We can brainstorm and collaborate more effectively. Team spirit and camaraderie flourish. And those who prefer on-site work report that they are more productive and collaborate better.

In-person interactions stimulate chemical reactions — the release of neurotransmitters such as dopamine and the hormone oxytocin reinforce the reward centers in our brains. These chemical responses and face-to-face social signals speed up our ability to convey empathy, trust and humor.

Also, from the employer's perspective, people coming in to the office has advantages. Managers can see if people are working, and they can interact with employees face to face. Plus, many companies have built offices that they need to justify keeping to shareholders.

In-person time vs. virtual time

Published studies shed some light on the different effects of virtual and in-person experiences. From our first interactions when we are born, we communicate using nonverbal cues in synchrony with others. In-person communication involves blending the timing of our gestures, words and movements. In videoconferences, whether conscious or not, we are trying to replicate that synchrony, which is impossible. Seeing someone on screen is certainly better than *not* seeing them. However, we don't really know when someone is multitasking and not giving us their full attention.

Dr. Jeremy Bailenson, professor and founding director at Stanford University's Virtual Human Interaction Lab, has highlighted several theories for why videoconferencing is less effective than meeting in person. He suggests that nonverbal overload — including unnatural eye gaze, cognitive load, looking at an all-day mirror of ourselves and greatly restricted mobility — contributes to "Zoom Fatigue."

Reinforcing the point, one experiment found that bonding between two people was greatest during in-person interaction, followed by video chat, audio chat and instant messaging — in that order. But the authors also found that pairs of people who used video chat more often reported greater bonding. When two people agree on the medium, bonding is potentially stronger.

A recent study published in the journal *Nature Human Behaviour* found that collaborative idea generation and creativity lessened when random pairs of people worked together virtually compared with when random pairs worked together in person. Another study reported that the shift to working from home corresponded with an increase in meetings and more time required to complete the same amount of work.

While technology saved us during the pandemic, it may have also slowed us down and separated us. Will this lead to a gradual deterioration in organizational culture? It has already begun.

CHAPTER 9
The Right Mix

In a June 2022 study of over 16,000 full-time U.S. employees, Gallup examined:

- various combinations of independent and collaborative working requirements
- the amount of in-office vs. remote time that maximized employee engagement and wellbeing and reduced burnout
- the likelihood that employees were looking for new jobs

Nearly nine in 10 (88%) of those in remote-ready jobs reported that they have a mix of independent and collaborative work; 61% said they perform their tasks independently and then later bring their work to the team for collaboration. Perhaps this was one of the big "Aha!" moments from the pandemic: Workers became aware that they could get a lot of their work done without being in the office every day.

We then asked people who had jobs that require collaboration how many days they were working at home and how many days they worked in the office. The sweet spot was two to three days in the office, which resulted in the best outcomes for employee engagement and wellbeing and for reducing job hunting and burnout. There was no discernable pattern between which *specific* days in the office and these outcomes. There was a slight lean toward people preferring to come in to the office on Tuesday, Wednesday and Thursday.

Outcomes were worse for those working all five days on-site, even after controlling for variation in job type. Full-time on-site employees were no more likely to say they feel like part of their organization's culture. As we will discuss later, while the number of days in the office matters, there are other factors that matter substantially more.

How to decide

In a 2022 in-depth study, Gallup asked remote-ready employees: *Who determines your hybrid work schedule?* Thirty-seven percent said it is entirely up to them, 26% said their employer or leadership decides, 24% said their manager or supervisor decides, and 13% said their work team decides together.

The option most associated with high levels of employee engagement — *my work team decides together* — was the one companies used the least.

A related point: Workers who reported that their employer required them to come in to the office on certain days — no matter the number — had lower engagement and wellbeing and higher burnout. They were also more likely to be looking for another job.

Employees crave autonomy, but they also want clarity. They want "smart autonomy" — autonomy that makes sense for how they can get their work done. What they *don't* want are general rules that don't make sense to them.

How then does an organization achieve smart autonomy? By managers leading discussions and asking employees to describe their work using questions like this:

- Which parts of your job can you do best at home?
- Which parts of your job can you do best at the office?
- When have you created exceptional value for our customers?
- When do you feel most connected to our organization's culture?

When asked where the best place for collaborative work is, 54% of employees say on-site or in the office, compared with only 15% who say at home or at another off-site location and 31%

> Employees crave **autonomy**, but they also want **clarity**.

who say there is no difference. Given this variance in how people collaborate, smart autonomy requires managers having the right conversations with their team members.

Finally, employees may not consider the impact that their choice to work remotely has on their coworkers. Managers need to coach employees to think beyond "Where I work is entirely up to me" — *because each employee has a responsibility to their team members and customers.*

CHAPTER 10
Splitters and Blenders: Two Different Relationships to Work

Consider how you would answer this question:

In your best life imaginable, would you prefer a job that is 9 to 5 where work and life are separated, or one where work and life are more blended throughout the day?

The former are work-life *splitters*, and the latter are work-life *blenders*. Among workers in the U.S., there is a dead-even tie between the two preferences. That seems surprising given the massive increase in hybrid work, which blends work and life more than ever for most jobs.

As organizations are deciding when and where people work, it is imperative that they know which of their employees are splitters and which are blenders.

Imagine managing someone and not knowing which type of employee they are.

Splitters might work best at home or in the office but want to maintain a *strict schedule* of hours in each location. Blenders might get their work done on weekends, evenings or early in the morning before the office opens.

Now imagine leading a team of people who don't know who the splitters are and who the blenders are on the team.

Splitters are more common in production jobs, but even 41% of them are blenders. Among other job types, it's closer to 50-50.

Splitters and Blenders by Job Type

Job type	n size	Splitters	Blenders
Production/Front line	883	59%	41%
White collar	3,510	47%	53%
Healthcare/Social assistance	738	46%	54%
Administrative/Clerical	580	48%	52%
Managerial	857	49%	51%
Other	797	47%	53%

Source: Gallup

Predictably, compared with other workers, on-site workers are more likely to be splitters, but still 39% of them prefer a blended work style.

Splitters and Blenders by Remote Work Status

Remote work status	n size	Splitters	Blenders
Exclusively remote	1,098	40%	60%
Hybrid	1,966	39%	61%
Exclusively on-site	3,128	61%	39%

Source: Gallup

Gen Z and young millennials are equally divided between splitters and blenders. More older millennials prefer blending work and life over splitting. As workers get older, they lean more toward wanting to split work and life, but 45% of working baby boomers prefer a work-life blend.

Splitters and Blenders by Generation

Generation (born during)	n size	Splitters	Blenders
Baby boomers (1946-1964)	2,510	55%	45%
Gen X (1965-1979)	2,803	52%	48%
Older millennials (1980-1988)	1,641	44%	56%
Gen Z and young millennials (1989 or after)	427	51%	49%

Source: Gallup

When Gallup studied the *outcomes* of splitters and blenders, we found that the percentage of engaged employees was the same for both groups — as were their overall levels of thriving and burnout.

Overall, blenders are more likely than splitters to be looking for another job (53% vs. 48%, respectively). This presents a slightly greater challenge for retaining these employees.

Managers need to ask their employees what their *best life imaginable* looks like. Are they splitters or blenders? For example, do they dislike getting emails on weekends or during off hours, or do they thrive on being constantly in the loop? Does it feel intrusive when their job disrupts their home life, or do they see work and life as seamless?

The reality is, both types of employees can be fulfilled, highly engaged and productive. But not knowing which is which could lead to lower engagement, feelings of disrespect and burnout.

CHAPTER 11
The Other Half — On-site Workers

Throughout this book, we focus on the new freedom that the remote-ready workforce is experiencing. We discuss how important autonomy is to employees and how leaders can work toward "smart autonomy."

However, about half of workers have jobs that they need to do on-site, such as manufacturing, transportation, healthcare, education and service. Many workers in those sectors might love the option to work from home but can't. Yet they want autonomy too. It is easy to imagine a psychological division between those who can work from home some of the time and those whose jobs require them to show up on-site every day. The latter may resent their colleagues who can fully enjoy the new freedom.

The question for organizational leaders is: *How do you give freedom to workers with 100% on-site jobs?*

Gallup recently asked CHROs of large global companies what flexibility options they were considering for their fully on-site employees. These were the most common options they suggested:

- work remotely some of the time
- work at multiple locations
- choice over hours they work (flextime)
- four-day workweeks (four 10-hour days)
- three-day workweeks
- flexible start and end times

- choice over which days they work per week
- choice over which hours they work per day
- shorter shift lengths
- increased paid time off (PTO) or vacation time
- relaxed dress code

We then asked on-site workers in the U.S. if their organization was offering those options. The most common response was relaxed dress code (55%), followed by flexible start and end times (33%) and choice over hours they work (flextime) (31%). We also asked employees which of these options they would change jobs to get. The two clear winners were not the ones organizations offered most: increased paid time off or vacation time (57%) and four-day workweeks (44%).

Vacations play an important role for organizations. They reduce dependence on any one associate and give employees a break from work. Gallup has found that people with more vacation time — controlling for other factors, including income — report higher wellbeing.

But people with engaging work and one week of vacation report 25% higher wellbeing than actively disengaged workers who have six or more weeks of vacation. While policies are important, *the quality of the work environment* has substantially greater impact than a specific policy.

The four-day workweek has gotten a lot of attention in the past few years. We'll look at that more closely in the next chapter.

CHAPTER 12
Is the Four-Day Workweek a Good Idea?

Amid disturbing levels of employee stress and burnout, some organizations are considering what might have been unthinkable a few years ago: reducing the workweek to four days.

The four-day workweek is a controversial idea, but is it a good one? Or are there better ways to promote worker wellbeing and productivity?

Some studies support reducing the number of hours worked each week. An experiment conducted in Iceland between 2015 and 2019 found that reducing hours while keeping pay the same increased productivity.

Researchers also reported that employees with a four-day workweek had lower burnout and higher wellbeing.

A similar work model — a four-day workweek trial — is being tested in Spain. In Japan, employers are urged to allow their employees to work four 10-hour days. And Scotland recently announced a policy to cut working hours by 20% without a decrease in pay.

Organizations are running their own experiments as well. A New Zealand company reduced employees' hours from 37.5 to 30 per week and allowed them to decide what days they would work. Another organization gave employees every other Friday off; according to the CEO, some workers enjoy using that day for individual "deep work," undistracted by meetings or calls.

As of this writing, the U.K. was in the midst of a six-month trial of the four-day workweek and its impact on employee wellbeing and productivity. Similar pilot studies are also taking place in Ireland, the U.S., Canada, Australia and New Zealand.

In June 2022, Gallup asked 12,313 full-time employees how many days they typically work in a week. For as much as it has been discussed, just 8% said they work four days a week — up from 5% in 2020 — while 84% said five days, and 8% said six days.

Gallup also collected employee engagement and wellbeing data for these employees. Overall, here's what we found:

- Those who work six days a week had the highest rates of burnout, the lowest percentage of thriving overall wellbeing and the highest active disengagement.
- Those who work five days a week had the highest engagement and lowest burnout rates.
- Those with four-day workweeks had the lowest active disengagement, but they did not have significantly higher thriving wellbeing compared with those who work five days a week. They also reported higher rates of burnout compared with those who work five days per week.

When Gallup studied these same patterns in March 2020, those with four-day workweeks reported significantly higher overall wellbeing than those with five-day workweeks. The gap has now closed.

Engagement, Wellbeing and Burnout by Number of Days Worked

Among U.S. employees who work 35+ hours per week

	Days typically worked per week		
Overall	Four	Five	Six
Engaged	28%	32%	30%
Actively disengaged	15%	17%	21%
Thriving wellbeing	56%	55%	45%
Feel burned out often/always	34%	29%	41%
Ratio of engaged to actively disengaged	1.9-to-1	1.9-to-1	1.4-to-1

	Days typically worked per week		
Fully on-site	Four	Five	Six
Engaged	25%	26%	25%
Actively disengaged	19%	23%	28%
Thriving wellbeing	57%	49%	37%
Feel burned out often/always	33%	31%	38%
Ratio of engaged to actively disengaged	1.3-to-1	1.1-to-1	0.9-to-1

Results control for differences in job types across employees

Source: Gallup Panel, June 2022

Our data suggest that a four-day workweek may be advantageous for those who do not have the option to work remotely. While it doesn't improve the likelihood that fully on-site workers will be engaged in their work or workplace, the four-day workweek does reduce the chance that they will perceive work as miserable — and increases their opportunity for thriving wellbeing. And as we noted in the previous chapter, as many as 44% of on-site employees would change jobs for a four-day workweek.

Debates over changing the workweek aren't new. In 1926, Ford Motor Company standardized a five-day workweek from the prevalent six-day workweek. Ford's leaders theorized that fewer days worked with the same pay would increase productivity through higher effort while at work.

But beneath the long-standing debate over the length of the workweek lies a deeper question about the nature of work itself. Consider these findings:

- Two-thirds or more of engaged employees are thriving in their overall lives regardless of how many days they work per week.

- An analysis of working populations in seven regions of the world found that for people with low job satisfaction and no opportunity to do what they do best, increasing the hours they worked led to declines in positive daily experiences and life evaluations. But the result was very different among employees with higher job satisfaction and an opportunity to do what they do best: Positive daily experiences and life evaluations did *not* substantially deteriorate when the number of hours they worked each day increased from five to 10.

- When it comes to overall wellbeing, the quality of the work experience has 2.5x to 3x the impact of the number of days or hours worked.

All of this complicates the question of whether implementing a four-day workweek is the right way to promote employee wellbeing.

If your goal is to build an engaging workplace culture, shortening the workweek may not be the best place to start. But it is an option that on-site employees say they would change jobs for, so you need to consider that in addition to the overall wellbeing benefits and reduction in work misery.

When it comes to overall wellbeing, the quality of the work experience has **2.5x to 3x the impact** of the number of days or hours worked.

While four-day workweeks may be a good idea for some individuals or organizations, policies that seek to control work-life "balance" are based on two dubious assumptions: that work is inevitably a bad thing, and that management knows what works best for *all* people.

The real problem is that *most employees are poorly managed.* Globally, nearly eight in 10 employees are not engaged or are actively disengaged at work. In the U.S., it's almost seven in 10. These people are spending their workday watching the clock, intentionally working against their employer or planning their escape — a symptom of an unhappy workplace.

If instead of shortening the workweek, employers focused on improving the *quality* of the work experience, they could nearly triple the positive influence on their employees' lives.

CHAPTER 13
The Reshuffling

The "Great Resignation" — when millions of people quit their jobs — emerged in 2021. It was predicted early that year — not by an economist, but by Anthony Klotz, at the time, a Texas A&M associate professor of management.

As of this writing, quit rates continue at high levels since Klotz's original prediction — some 4 million voluntary quits per month in the U.S.

Klotz's forecast of surging quit rates was rooted in his hypothesis that the poor job market associated with the pandemic led to "pent-up resignations." During the first part of the pandemic, people chose to keep their jobs during layoffs and furloughs even if those jobs were uninspiring, and they let feelings of dissatisfaction simmer until the job market improved.

This isn't surprising. People tend to choose stability in times of crisis. But employees also had time to evaluate what they really wanted from work. Amid a global pandemic that created anxiety and stress and reminded them of their mortality, they reconsidered their work life.

Gallup reported two trends that provide further insight into why record numbers of people left their jobs. First, pent-up demand for new jobs met opportunity. In January 2020, 68% of Americans said it was a good time to find a job. That percentage tanked to 22% in April and continued in the 20%-30% range through January of 2021. In April 2021, it rose to 43% and peaked at 74% in October 2021 — and is now in the 60s. These figures track with the large shift in quit rates.

The second trend: Discontented, disengaged workers acted on their unhappiness and decreasing commitment to their employers — some of which they had been feeling for years. At the same time, *engaged* employees actually became *more committed* to their organizations.

Gallup found that people who were either actively disengaged or not engaged in their jobs — those who already felt discontentment at work before the pandemic hit — were more likely to be actively looking for jobs or watching for job openings.

As COVID-19 wore on through 2021, this gap widened. Discontented employees were *even more likely* to be looking for new work, while engaged employees were *increasingly less likely* to be actively looking for work.

The changing job market also caused discontented employees to become even less loyal. Gallup found a parallel phenomenon during the recessions of 2001-2002 and 2008-2009: The relationship between employee engagement and business outcomes, including employee retention, is even stronger during tough times.

It might have been more accurate to call the Great Resignation the **"Great Reshuffling."**

Discontented Employees Are Becoming Less Loyal

Percentage likely to leave

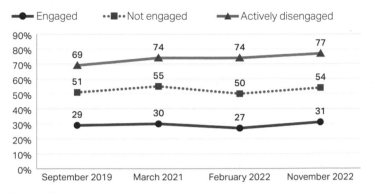

Source: Gallup

When we look more closely at the U.S. Bureau of Labor Statistics' economic data, quit rates don't tell the full story. Hiring rates also continued to rise. People simply changed employers instead of dropping out of the workforce altogether. It might have been more accurate to call the Great Resignation the "Great Reshuffling."

The industries hit hardest by turnover were manufacturing, transportation, utilities, trade, retail, healthcare and accommodations/food services. Job openings in these industries also continued to increase, and hiring rates haven't kept up. As of this writing, in the employer-employee power dynamic, the power is squarely in the hands of the employee. Even in a recession, that dynamic may not change if the gap between job openings and hiring rates remains substantial.

Why employees leave and what they're looking for

During 2021, Gallup asked employees why they left their employer and what would attract them to a new employer. While pay and benefits were the top reasons employees gave for leaving, only 14% of respondents mentioned them.

About three-fourths of the top reasons employees gave for leaving their employer were related to either employee engagement and culture (47%) — advancement and development opportunities, not being treated with respect, unrealistic job expectations and responsibilities, and the job not being a good fit — or wellbeing (27%) — relocation, work-life balance, personal reasons and work schedule.

What attracts people to new employers? Income, greater work-life balance, a job that allows them to do what they do best, and greater stability and job security — over half of respondents said these factors were very important in a new employer.

Gallup has found that income, while it tops the importance list, is nuanced. The amount of money the average employee requires to change employers depends on their current salary. For example, $10,000 has a different meaning for someone with a low salary than for someone with a high salary. Employees make decisions based on the *percentage* increase in salary, in addition to their level of engagement.

Most employees require as much as a 20% income increase to change jobs. This is particularly the case for discontented workers — 73% of actively disengaged employees would leave for a 20% increase or less. Engaged employees require, on average, a 31% increase in pay to change jobs.

New job opportunities may have sparked the Great Resignation — or Great Reshuffling. But the real catalyst was a workforce that thought more deeply about their jobs and the role work plays in their lives and wellbeing.

CHAPTER 14
In Decline: Employee Engagement

Strong measures of employee engagement include elements that improve work life *and* predict business outcomes — notably, customer retention, but also productivity, employee retention, safety and profitability, according to Gallup's meta-analytics of 112,312 business units and teams in 96 countries.

We found that engaged employees:

- are 2x as likely to be thriving in their lives
- can see opportunities for growth and development
- put in extra effort to create exceptional customer value
- feel connected to the mission and purpose of the organization
- have coworkers they collaborate with
- are more resilient during hard times

So how are the world's organizations doing since the pandemic on engaging their employees and building a workforce that can create exceptional customer value? Not well.

After trending up for a decade starting at 12% in 2009, employee engagement globally slipped from 22% in 2019 to 20% in 2020 and reached a high of 23% in 2022. Gallup's annual *State of the Global Workplace* study reports variance in the percentage of engaged employees across regions and countries around the world — with a high of 32% in the U.S. and a low of only 14% in Europe. Gallup estimates that low employee engagement costs the global economy $7.8 trillion in lost productivity — a staggering 11% of global GDP.

Even the country with the most engaged employees, the U.S., saw its first annual decline in a decade. Starting at 26% in 2000, the percentage of engaged employees in the U.S. did not have much movement through 2010 and reached a high of 36% in 2020 — then dropped to 34% in 2021. This downward pattern continued into 2022, when only 32% of U.S. employees were engaged.

U.S. and Global Employee Engagement Trends

Percentage engaged

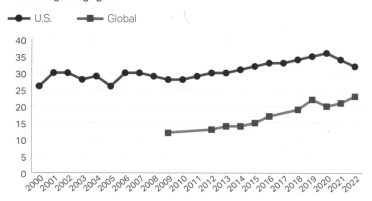

Percentages for global and U.S. engagement trends are calculated using annual data from Gallup random samples of the working population.

Source: Gallup

Some of the reasons for the recent declines in engagement are obvious. The pandemic disrupted how people work, and leaders and managers had to anticipate and respond to pandemic spikes.

Trying to blend work and life — managers and employees trying to manage their lives at the same time they were managing work — has also been disruptive. Burnout among managers rose significantly.

Uncertainty contributes to disengagement

Gallup saw the most decline in agreement with these engagement (Q^{12}) items from early 2021 to 2022:

- I know what is expected of me at work.
- At work, I have the opportunity to do what I do best every day.
- I have the materials and equipment I need to do my work right.
- The mission or purpose of my company makes me feel my job is important.

We also found an eight-point decrease in the percentage of employees who were extremely satisfied with their organization as a place to work.

Healthcare workers had the greatest drop in engagement (nine points) from early 2021 to early 2022. Managers' engagement fell seven points from early to late 2021, and as noted above, manager burnout spiked.

Since before the pandemic, declining engagement was evident across employees who were exclusively remote, hybrid and exclusively on-site — but the decline was greatest for exclusively remote employees.

Why engagement is even more important now

With the increases in hybrid and fully remote work, many have asked Gallup if the same employee engagement elements are relevant. Gallup studied how each of the 12 engagement items predict outcomes such as job hunting, likelihood to recommend and burnout.

Gallup compared the impact of employee engagement before the pandemic to its impact in 2022, after the workplace shifted. Two distinct patterns emerged: Engagement items related to role clarity (*knowing what is expected* and *having the opportunity to do what you do best*) and coworker relationships (*fellow associates are committed to doing quality work* and *having a best friend at work*) mattered *even more* than before the pandemic.

To illustrate, before the pandemic, those with a best friend at work were 50% more likely than others to strongly recommend their company as a place to work and 13% less likely to leave their organization. In 2022, those with a best friend at work were twice as likely to strongly recommend their company and 24% less likely to leave their organization.

Gallup's time-tested 12 employee engagement question items represent basic human needs at work. But as times change, work priorities change — in this case, role clarity and workplace relationships.

Employee engagement is foundational to improving the wellbeing, resilience and customer focus of a workforce because it includes elements of communication, development and collaboration. These elements set the stage for trust and overall wellbeing.

CHAPTER 15
The Risk of Not Caring About Employee Wellbeing

Why would anyone put in extra effort if they feel like you don't care about them?

Only about one in four U.S. employees feel strongly that their organization cares about their wellbeing. This percentage has been trending down since it peaked at the start of the pandemic. Gallup has found similarly low numbers in Germany, France and the U.K.

This finding has significant implications now that work and life are more blended than ever before.

As we noted earlier, those who prefer remote work cite reduced commute times, flexibility for their family and their *wellbeing* as some of the key reasons.

In 2011, long before the pandemic, about the same percentage of U.S. employees strongly agreed that their employer cared about their overall wellbeing (21%).

Then at the onset of the pandemic in 2020, employers responded quickly with plans, communication and what many employees believed was genuine concern for them. And the percentage who felt their organization cared

Employees' expectations have fundamentally changed since 2020.

about them nearly doubled, reaching a high of 49% in May of that year. But since 2020, the percentage has plummeted to the previous low levels.

U.S. Employee Perceptions of Organization Caring About Their Wellbeing

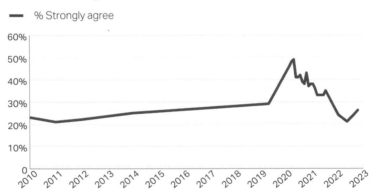

Percentage of employees who strongly agree with this statement: My organization cares about my overall wellbeing.

Source: Gallup

78

Why it matters

Employees who strongly agree that their employer cares about their overall wellbeing, compared with those who don't, are:

- 3x more likely to be engaged at work
- 69% less likely to actively search for a new job
- 71% less likely to report experiencing a lot of burnout
- 5x more likely to strongly advocate for their company as a place to work
- 5x more likely to strongly agree that they trust the leadership of their organization
- 36% more likely to be thriving in their overall lives

Gallup has also found that teams most likely to feel like the organization cares about their wellbeing have higher customer engagement, profitability and productivity; lower turnover; and fewer safety incidents.

Employees' expectations have fundamentally changed since 2020. Many employees now have new and more serious factors to consider when they think about their job, including if their employer cares about their wellbeing. The intersection between work and life has new meaning — upping the bar for employers.

CHAPTER 16
Increasing Employee-Employer Disconnect

Declining levels of employee engagement and feeling like their employer cares about their wellbeing — and increasing levels of dissatisfaction — are signs of a growing disconnect between employees and employers. The expectations of the new workforce don't match the actual *experience* employees have at work.

Ultimately, this disconnect has serious implications for customer retention. Earlier, we highlighted the recent decline in the American Customer Satisfaction Index, which measures customers' satisfaction with company products and services — how close they are to ideal and the extent to which they meet or exceed expectations.

From 2020 to 2022, among exclusively remote employees of all ages, we saw a significant drop in the percentage who say that they are *extremely proud* of the quality of the products and services their organization offers. This is especially true for workers below age 35, regardless of whether they work remotely, on-site or hybrid and for workers 35 and older who are exclusively remote. Younger employees are also less likely to feel great responsibility for the quality of their organization's products and services.

Pride in Organization's Products and Services Drops From 2020 to 2022 Among Most Employees

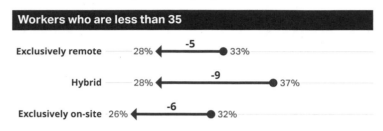

Percentage of employees who strongly agree with this statement: I'm extremely proud of the quality of products/services my organization offers.

Source: Gallup

Only one in five employees strongly agree that the leadership of their organization makes decisions that are in the customers' best interest. This perception is highly correlated with delivering on promises to customers. Why would employees care if their leaders don't care?

Consider this:

- Engaged employees are 4x as likely to feel extremely proud of the products and services their organization offers.
- Employees who experience frequent or constant burnout are 50% less likely to feel that their organization always delivers on its promise to customers.
- Among U.S. workers, approval of labor unions is at its highest point since 1965 (71%) — and the younger the worker, the more interested they are in joining a union.

These facts indicate that employees are becoming dangerously alienated from their employers. And the consequences of employee-employer detachment include less commitment and effort from employees to go the extra mile for customers, less loyalty to the organization, and higher turnover.

CHAPTER 17
How to Win in the New Environment

Only 21% of global and 32% of U.S. employees are engaged. But here's the good news: Some organizations have achieved 13x the global engagement average.

Each year, Gallup identifies organizations that beat the overall engagement average, create exceptional cultures and deliver superior customer value. These organizations averaged 70% or more engaged employees even during a highly disruptive 2021 and 2022.

The best-run organizations build cultures where employees feel like leadership genuinely cares about them. These organizations have at least six in 10 employees who say they strongly agree that their organization cares about their overall wellbeing.

> The best-run organizations build cultures where **employees feel like leadership genuinely cares about them.**

Here's what they do differently:

- build trust in leadership by making decisions that reflect the organization's values
- embrace flexible work environments while developing plans for the future
- take employee wellbeing (mental health) seriously
- use transparent and creative multichannel communication with employees and customers (e.g., podcasts, a company app, virtual town halls, YouTube)
- upskill managers to coach through times of change so they are equipped to manage performance effectively and so they can be the key conduit for progress on the four items above

The pandemic caused a "great forced experiment" that gave organizations and employees an opportunity to learn what worked and what didn't.

PART 3
Strengths to Role

CHAPTER 18
How Do We Know if Employees Are Productive?

> Why is it that we often design organizations as if people naturally shirk responsibility, do only what is required, resist learning, and can't be trusted to do the right thing?
>
> — Abraham Maslow

We don't know if Maslow's question decades ago was rhetorical. But we do know that it remains as relevant as ever. With the recent increase in remote working, organizational leaders started asking the same question: *How do we know if our employees are working and productive?* The question assumes that the only way leaders can know if people are productive is if they can see them physically in the office.

Leaders' assumptions about human intentions are central to most decisions, especially about rules and policies. How they manage and develop people is contingent on an essential question about human nature: *Are people trustworthy and eager to work and learn, or not?* How many leaders have even asked themselves this question? How often are programs and practices put into place without considering this question, but intending to control employees who — presumably — cannot be trusted?

Consider the temptation to exert control these past few years with the surge in hybrid and fully remote work and leaders not seeing employees on a regular basis. Essentially, the number of people in remote-ready jobs working in either hybrid or fully remote locations doubled.

Leader control has been gradually eroding for centuries, starting with the Industrial Revolution. But with increases in quit rates in 2021 and 2022, leader control hit a new low. New freedom, low unemployment and more job openings caused employees to be selective about where and how they work.

How leaders manage and develop people is contingent on an essential question about human nature: **Are people trustworthy and eager to work and learn, or not?**

The evolution of people management

Prior to the 19th century, most businesses were relatively small. A business owner might manage some family members and a few other employees in a specialized craft. The Industrial Revolution changed that. Larger organizations were formed to mass produce goods in manufacturing and industrial plants. These large organizations needed structures so business owners could manage the large number of people.

In the late 1800s and early 1900s, the discipline of management started appearing in higher education. Later, in the mid-20th century, "scientific management" became more prominent through methods such as reengineering and Six Sigma. Psychologists and sociologists entered the mix and began developing new theories for managing people.

In practice, people management was mostly command and control, even though some scholars were theorizing that a "participative" approach to managing might work best. With the growth of the information age, people accumulated knowledge and expertise — and they would take that expertise with them when they changed companies.

Different theories for how to manage people emerged.

In the 1950s and 1960s, Douglas McGregor, a professor at MIT and one of Maslow's collaborators, created a theoretical fork in the road when he described two approaches to management: Theory X and Theory Y. Theory X posits that the average employee is not ambitious or highly responsible and is mainly motivated by rewards and punishments — people are extrinsically motivated, the theory goes. The management style for those who subscribe to Theory X is command and control, or micromanagement.

Theory Y takes the view that the average employee is self-motivated, responsible and fulfilled by the work itself — they are intrinsically motivated. The management style for those who endorse Theory Y is to involve employees and encourage them to take ownership of their work. These managers tend to get to know employees on a more personal level than Theory X managers.

Which theory is right?

Meta-analyses published in the management literature illustrate that both styles can get results — but *different* results. Extrinsic rewards associated with Theory X management tend to motivate the specific behaviors that are being rewarded or punished. Whereas intrinsic rewards associated with Theory Y — such as engaging and fulfilling work — tend to broaden thinking and decision-making. Intrinsic rewards are more common in knowledge jobs, in which employees are expected to use some amount of discretionary judgment — such as spontaneously helping a customer, looking out for a coworker or combining information in a new way to improve the overall organization.

Some would conclude that a combination of Theory X and Theory Y is best, depending on the situation. But one thing is clear in today's world of work: An organization is at risk if it doesn't emphasize Theory Y management.

Which theory do leaders really believe? The evidence to date suggests that most organizations are still being run as if they subscribe to Theory X. For example, only one in four workers globally strongly agree that their opinions seem to count at work. The simple habit of listening to people who are close to the action is missing in most organizations.

A 2022 Gallup-Workhuman study found that recognition and praise for good work predicts higher employee engagement, advocacy for the organization and intentions to stay with the organization. But eight in 10 senior leaders (81%) say recognition is a not major strategic priority.

The economic environment also matters. When unemployment is high, leaders have more control. But they have far less control in tight job markets with many job openings, as we saw in 2021 and 2022. The irony is, Gallup has found that employee engagement has an even stronger impact on performance outcomes, such as customer loyalty and profit, during tough economic times (e.g., a recession) when leaders have *more* control.

While leaders need to make tough decisions — sometimes decisions employee don't like — leading with command and control doesn't work very well in the new workforce.

CHAPTER 19
Systems That Work Against Human Nature

With the rise of the Industrial Revolution, standardized process efficiencies through automation — factories, mills, quality control, accounting and workflow planning — brought conveniences, cost efficiencies and better overall lives for everyone.

The goal of many early management thinkers such as Adam Smith, Frederick Winslow Taylor, Henry Gantt, Frank and Lillian Galbreth, and Herbert Townes was to increase the efficiency and consistency of production, reduce variation, and make processes more predictable with fewer errors.

Leaders could only be as effective as their managers, so giving managers a process to follow was essential. Process efficiency was integrated into how people were managed — find defects and correct weaknesses.

Human progress developed quickly through the Industrial Revolution, but *human development* didn't.

In designing the processes that led to production efficiency, leaders took advantage of one of human nature's greatest strengths: Our brains are hardwired to critique and find fault. Defect reduction is critical, particularly in environments where lives and safety are at stake. In more modern workplaces, managers write up annual employee reviews, and the first instinct is to focus on failures or "opportunities for improvement."

Human progress developed quickly through the Industrial Revolution, but **human development didn't.**

Traditional performance management is set up to rate and rank employees and focus primarily on their weaknesses. But this approach fails to improve performance. Just 19% of employees strongly agree that how they are managed motivates them to do outstanding work.

We may be naturally wired to give criticism, but we sure aren't wired to receive it. We crave praise any time we can get it. Constant criticism makes it nearly impossible for a manager and employee to build a healthy relationship.

What is the right balance between praise and criticism?

Critical feedback is necessary, and everyone needs to be aware and accountable for their shortcomings. But to inspire great performance, managers must lead with meaningful feedback that's grounded in team members' strengths. This simple starting point builds trust and increases the chance that critical feedback will turn into real development.

And no matter how many studies have been conducted illustrating the impact of humanistic (positive) psychology, it has remained easier for mainstream leaders and managers to try to inspire their workforces using systems that assume people operate like machines and that everyone develops in the same way.

How then should managers structure the "ideal" day for employees to encourage higher engagement and performance?

Today's workers expect their manager to coach them — primarily based on their strengths.

Coaching managers change the starting point from this: *We are all the same, develop in the same way and need to be well-rounded* to this: *We all have our own unique innate talents that can be turned into exceptional competencies.*

In a study conducted years before the COVID-19 pandemic, Gallup asked employees to review their most recent workday and to report the number of hours they spent doing various activities. What best differentiated engaged from actively disengaged (miserable) employees was how much time they spent using their strengths — feeling so absorbed in their work that they experienced timelessness and flow.

Engaged employees spent 4x as much time using their strengths compared with what they don't do well. Miserable employees spent about equal time using their strengths and weaknesses.

Gallup replicated the study above in 2022. We again asked employees to reflect on their most recent workday and found that strengths mattered *even more* in today's workplaces. In 2022, engaged employees spent 5x as much time using their strengths compared with what they don't do well. Miserable employees still spent about equal time on their strengths and weaknesses.

Engaged employees aren't immune to negativity or job stress. Gallup research shows that engaged or not, employees experience *more stress* during the workweek than on the weekend. That's not surprising. Most employees deal with unexpected requests and workplace drama all the time.

A strengths approach to performance is not about glossing over weaknesses or making sure employees get to work on *only* assignments and projects they like. Everyone's role includes tasks that aren't much fun.

Likewise, there will be times when managers need to give employees constructive feedback to help them improve in their roles. But when managers treat feedback like it's a balancing act, performance management falters. They shouldn't spend equal time on criticism and praise. The scales should be heavily tilted toward what employees do best.

Peter Drucker, Abraham Maslow and Don Clifton came to the same conclusion about human development in organizations: People develop best when they have opportunities to use their strengths. While their professional careers overlapped by almost five decades, these strengths pioneers took different paths to finding this essential truth.

CHAPTER 20
Strengths Pioneer — Peter Drucker

> **A person can perform only from strength.**
>
> — Peter Drucker (1909-2005)

Peter Drucker, commonly known as the founder of modern management, spent six decades examining how organizations function — resulting in 39 books, hundreds of articles and the development of management education.

His writings included many accurate predictions, including the emergence of privatization, decentralization, the rise of Japan as an economic power and the impact of marketing. In 1959, he predicted that "the information age" would change how people worked, and he coined the term "knowledge worker." Drucker foresaw that jobs would evolve beyond routine labor to increasingly require decision-making, improvisation and judgment.

There are now more than 1 billion knowledge workers globally. Even jobs not technically classified as knowledge work such as production and manufacturing have aspects of knowledge work — where discretionary effort plays a role.

Drucker famously developed "Management by Objectives" (MBO), an approach in which management and employees work together to set objectives and goals. In essence, employees play an active role in goal setting, progress discussions and rewards. A meta-analysis published in the *Journal of Applied Psychology* found that CEOs who practiced MBO achieved a 56% gain in productivity compared with those who didn't emphasize MBO; the latter had a 6% gain.

As Drucker's thinking evolved, he came to the realization that organizations function best when employees use their strengths. His discovery of the importance of strengths management was informed by his long-term observations of successful organizations that then led him to study individual success within organizations. Drucker had a top-down approach.

Abraham Maslow and Don Clifton discovered the importance of strengths management by first studying how individuals function best and then applying that knowledge to organizations — a bottom-up approach.

CHAPTER 21
Strengths Pioneer — Abraham Maslow

> What a man can be, he must be.
> He must be true to his own nature.
>
> — Abraham Maslow (1908-1970)

While most famous for developing a hierarchy of human needs, Abraham Maslow was one of the founders of the field known today as humanistic or positive psychology — the study of optimum human functioning — which was in direct contrast to behaviorism and Freudian psychology that focused more on dysfunction.

Maslow was a keen observer of successful individuals and "peak experiences." His hierarchy of human needs describes how people can move from basic physiological and safety needs to higher-level belonging and confidence needs to the highest need of self-actualization. Self-actualization includes fulfilling your greatest potential through your talents. While the legacy of Maslow's work and hierarchy of human needs is significant, it does not fully represent his contributions to the field of management.

Later in his career, Maslow came to the realization that a person's work and life experiences are even more important than their education. He began applying his discoveries of individual self-actualization to management.

Maslow and Drucker read each other's works. Drucker endorsed Maslow's book on management saying it had "a lasting impact on me." Maslow found that a person can only reach their full potential in life if they are doing what they do best. Self-actualization doesn't just hit people like a lightning bolt. They earn it through hard work in an area of their natural talent.

Maslow concluded that great communities, well-run organizations and good teams could have more impact on an individual than one-on-one interactions with a therapist. While Drucker studied the impact of business on society, Maslow emphasized how a job with the right fit could affect society: Truly fulfilled people were those who worked on something they considered important, which influenced how they treated others and how much they contributed to their communities.

Maslow's intuitions were right. Gallup research has found that globally, countries with more engaged workers have more people who are willing to help a stranger in need. Countries with more disengaged workers are home to people who are less likely to donate to charities.

Maslow changed the world of management through a paradigm shift from a focus on what is wrong with people to one that emphasizes the value of self-actualization, especially through work.

Don Clifton, who knew Drucker and closely followed the work of Maslow, took a somewhat different approach. He developed a measurement-based system that would later revolutionize individual development. The seeds of Clifton's strengths journey were planted very early.

CHAPTER 22
Strengths Pioneer — Don Clifton

> What would happen if we studied what was *right* with people?
>
> — Don Clifton (1924-2003)

This simple question, posed six decades ago by Don Clifton, launched the global strengths movement.

The question was particularly personal for Clifton.

During World War II, he put his mathematics skills to the test as an Army Air Force navigator flying on B-24s. While flying over the Azores in bad weather, his flight went off course. Clifton had a hunch about how to correct it. But when he did the math, he realized his intuition was wrong. He learned to trust science over personal intuition.

Clifton received the Distinguished Flying Cross for heroism during his 25 successful bombing sorties. But when he returned home from WWII, he had seen enough war and destruction. He wanted to spend the rest of his life doing good for humankind. This led to his intense interest in studying human development in a different way — studying what was *right* with people.

In 1949, Clifton and his colleagues started the Nebraska Human Resources Research Foundation at the University of Nebraska. The foundation served as a community service for students and as a laboratory for graduate students to practice strengths-based psychology. Clifton and his students and colleagues discovered that successful students — those who persisted to graduation — had notably different character traits than less successful ones.

These early discoveries about successful people stirred other hypotheses. Clifton and his colleagues began to study the most successful school counselors, teachers, salespeople and managers. Clifton discovered that successful people in specific roles shared certain traits. He defined those tendencies as "naturally recurring patterns of thought, feeling or behavior that can be productively applied."

Clifton wanted to identify universal but practical traits that were predictive of high-performance outcomes. And he wanted to identify tendencies that were unique to each individual but that could be developed into strengths with practice. The purpose of this work was to bring focus to conversations so people could better understand not just who they are — but what they could become.

Clifton developed hundreds of predictive instruments that identified top performers for specific jobs within an organization's unique culture. These scientifically validated instruments found the best talent fit for the right position in a specific company.

But there was something missing.

The ability to identify great talent for an organization was not always helpful to individuals. So, in the mid-1990s, Clifton developed an assessment that identified specific traits and a framework for developing those traits for the benefit of individuals. He labeled those traits "strengths."

Along his journey to create what would become the CliftonStrengths assessment, Clifton met with many academics and fellow researchers. Perhaps the most significant connection was with Harvard psychology professor Phil Stone.

Stone was an advocate for a newly discovered technology called "the internet." Stone's two recommendations for Clifton were to build the assessment for the coming digital age and to use a modified ipsative scoring algorithm, rather than the customary normative scoring, as in the Likert scale (1-5) or multiple choice. Ipsative scoring asks a respondent to choose between two socially desirable outcomes. It is based on the assumption that individuals are often presented with multiple positive alternatives in real-life situations — for example, "I organize" and "I analyze." Ipsative measurement is particularly useful in identifying intrapersonal characteristics — it reduces social desirability bias, or "gaming," that can happen with many normative measurements.

Clifton distilled all of these research findings into the original 34 strengths themes that became StrengthsFinder and later CliftonStrengths.

His work has inspired books read by millions around the world, including *Soar With Your Strengths*, which Clifton coauthored with Paula Nelson; *Strengths Based Leadership*; *Now, Discover Your Strengths*; and one of the bestselling business books of all time, *StrengthsFinder 2.0*.

Near the end of his life, Clifton was honored with a Presidential Commendation by the American Psychological Association as the Father of Strengths-Based Psychology.

His mission upon returning from World War II was to make a significant contribution to human development. As of this writing, nearly 30 million people have discovered their CliftonStrengths.

Clifton changed the world by creating a taxonomy of strengths that is being used all around the world.

The 34 CliftonStrengths Themes

- Achiever
- Activator
- Adaptability
- Analytical
- Arranger
- Belief
- Command
- Communication
- Competition
- Connectedness
- Consistency
- Context
- Deliberative
- Developer
- Discipline
- Empathy
- Focus
- Futuristic
- Harmony
- Ideation
- Includer
- Individualization
- Input
- Intellection
- Learner
- Maximizer
- Positivity
- Relator
- Responsibility
- Restorative
- Self-Assurance
- Significance
- Strategic
- Woo

CHAPTER 23
Fitting Strengths to Role at the Highest Leadership Levels

> One cannot build performance on weakness, let alone on something one cannot do at all.
>
> — Peter Drucker

A global organization had a London location that was failing its customers badly. Customer retention had become a serious problem. The office needed a fix-it leader, or it would go broke.

The same organization had an office in Singapore that was well-run and had valuable client relationships but desperately needed new business. The organization needed to reintroduce itself and its products throughout the region. This office needed a rainmaker leader to restart it.

There were two very good internal candidates for the roles; both were proven winners in the organization. They were each at a critical moment in their careers and ready for their next big advancement in leadership. On the surface, either should have done well in either job. However, a closer look at the candidates — Deepak and Jenny — reveals two very different strengths profiles.

Deepak's CliftonStrengths profile shows that he leads with Restorative, Maximizer, Responsibility and Self-Assurance. (See Chapter 22 for a list of the 34 CliftonStrengths themes.) He is a classic fixer. He lives to solve problems — the harder, the better. He is fearless when confronted with frustrated clients because with his Self-Assurance, he knows he will win the day.

Deepak has no anxiety about difficult situations because he knows once he understands the problem, he can fix anything. He can't wait to confront a problem. Deepak is a rare talent — he is a world-class fix-it guy.

Jenny leads with Futuristic, Competition, Individualization and Woo. She loves to win over senior executives she has never met. She sees the solution to all problems through the lens of winning a big deal.

Jenny wraps up all strategy sessions with the same conclusion: "We need to throw long." She gets up early knowing that she will walk into a boardroom full of people she has never met and must win the room. To many executives, this is a high-anxiety situation. Jenny is different. She can't wait to get there. She doesn't worry about her presentation over the weekend, and knowing it is coming up energizes her. Jenny is a rare talent — she is a rainmaker.

Here is what we need to know: Unlike Jenny, Deepak is uncomfortable meeting people he doesn't have some previous connection with. It creates anxiety and avoidance for him — and overpowers his rare fix-it talents. During strengths coaching, Deepak says that while he will walk through any door in the world if there is a problem to solve, he dreads walking through first-impression doors. He worries about that kind of meeting, and way down deep, hopes the day will never come.

Jenny, with all her superpowers, is just the opposite. She dreads client meetings that demand fixing hard problems. She thinks about them over the weekend and hopes the day will never come. In a fix-it meeting, her talents never come up. She experiences cognitive narrowing and becomes less creative and spontaneous.

She suddenly appears *not* to be very talented. This star rainmaker's superpowers don't come through in that moment.

Both Deepak and Jenny are five-star players, but in the wrong role, they would fail — or at minimum, never soar. Their careers were on the line. So was the company's stock price.

The organization came up with a solution that was a game changer. It assigned fix-it Deepak to London, which was failing customers and had a huge problem to fix. And rainmaker Jenny went to Singapore, which desperately needed new customers. Fitting both of their strengths profiles to the right roles grew the company's revenue, earnings and stock price. This was the ultimate "strengths to role" executive decision. And it changed the overall company value as much or more than an acquisition of a competitor.

CHAPTER 24
Coaching Strengths to Role at the Highest Leadership Levels

Unlike Deepak and Jenny, Giselle found herself in what seemed to be the wrong role for her, and she feared she was doomed to fail. But with good coaching on her strengths, she found a way to thrive in the role.

Giselle landed a job as top executive of a division in a famous media company. She was eager to lead the department to new heights. When she got there, it turned out the job primarily required high-level sales activities, which the company had neglected to make clear to her. She was the top executive of this division and needed sales success or there would be no projects and no new revenue. This was a serious career and life crisis for Giselle because she is a horrible salesperson.

Giselle's obstacle was that she hated cold calling. The thought of calling organizations where she didn't know anyone every day made her sick to her stomach. Her confidence and spontaneity shut down when she had to make a sales presentation. This one talent barrier would surely cause her to fail at her new job.

One of her strengths, however, was that she loved communicating hard concepts to people. She thrived when she was helping people understand complicated current events that affect their own jobs as well as their organizations' future. She loved to read everything and then help very smart people understand concepts they had never previously understood. When she saw their light go on, that was her money moment.

Giselle reached out to a longtime mentor for some feedback and coaching. Her mentor said to her, "Why don't you perform the sales role of your new leadership job by helping prospects and clients understand difficult concepts — ones they thought they could never understand — just like you do with me? When you get to the prospect meeting, sell by using your natural strengths instead of pretending you are a world-class salesperson. Just start *teaching* them rather than selling them. Just start helping them learn something that they really need to know."

He went on to advise, "Influence them through your Learner, Communication, Self-Assurance and Individualization strengths. Teach them something that helps them do their job better, and they will never quit seeking your advice and services."

Giselle took his advice, and her department's revenues exploded. She needed to hire 100 new professionals. When onlookers saw her doing her job, they said, "Giselle is a talented leader with masterful sales ability — she can run anything."

Her career took off not because of her expertise in sales, but because she masterfully fit her teaching strengths to the role.

The reality is that Giselle had the potential to become a strong leader using her strengths. But she would have missed that opportunity because she was viewing one task — sales — through a traditional lens of "selling" skills. Giselle soared as a leader because she used her strengths in a nontraditional way to rise up and win.

There is always a strengths-to-role strategy to win at work and life — even at the highest levels.

CHAPTER 25
Why Build a Strengths-Based Culture?

With the workplace shifting to more hybrid and remote work, organizations need effective and efficient collaboration now more than ever. They need a common language that quickly familiarizes employees, managers and leaders with each other. Strengths is that language.

For example, if we know someone has high Activator, we can appreciate their natural ability to get a project started fast and understand why they sometimes can be impatient. If we know someone is talented in the Deliberative theme, we can recognize their thoughtfulness in resolving a customer issue rather than hold their slow, methodical behavior against them.

Diversity of strengths is an advantage

For thousands of years, we have been aware of the innate differences between individuals we work and live with. Even within the close genetic pools of families, personalities and other traits differ greatly. Ancient tribes were made up of people with widely varying innate tendencies — some better at making new friends, some with superior problem-solving skills, some with great command to lead and some who loved getting things done every day. These differences, when put to use, were invaluable to the survival, resiliency and longevity of the tribe.

If someone had documented the successes and failures of communities over the last 10,000 years, we would have had an enormous database to make sense of how people work best in groups. Now we know.

- In one recent study, Gallup analysts collected data from 11,441 teams across six industries. The teams varied from 0% to 100% of team members knowing their strengths via the CliftonStrengths assessment. We also collected employee engagement and performance data from each team. Our biggest meta-analysis discovery was that a team's *awareness* of its strengths is a better indicator of engagement and performance than the *specific composition* of the strengths. Teams with 90% or more team members knowing their strengths had the best outcomes.

- Groups that receive strengths interventions have substantially lower turnover and achieve higher sales, profit, customer engagement and employee engagement, based on meta-analysis of 103 studies in 11 industries, 111 countries and across 20,021 teams.

The overarching goal of a strengths-based organization is to build a customer-centric culture where individuals use their unique differences to make the overall organization more productive. Strengths-based organizations significantly increase the odds that employees and customers will be engaged, thriving and have good mental health.

So what does a strengths-based culture look like? Here are some signs:

- Individual employees strongly agree that they have the opportunity to do what they do best every day.
- Team members can name and understand the individual strengths of everyone on the team.
- Team members can see the link between strengths and success, such as improvements in competencies, performance and customer service.
- Everyone on the team has partnerships that encourage their strengths development.
- Team members use their knowledge of each other's strengths to plan and direct their actions.
- Managers use individual strengths to set meaningful goals and clarify expectations with each employee.
- Managers know how each team member's strengths connect to the role they play.
- Teams are more agile in responding to customer needs.

In the next chapter, we will discuss how to build a strengths-based culture.

CHAPTER 26
Steps to Building a Strengths-Based Culture

Very few organizations in the world can say their culture is "strengths-based." This is a missed opportunity. Organizations with strengths-based cultures greatly outperform their competitors by building much stronger customer relationships.

Building a strengths-based culture is hard work. Simply knowing everyone's strengths is not enough. It takes conversations, coaching and practice to successfully integrate strengths into daily routines. The most effective way to accomplish this is by systematically upskilling your managers and certifying them to coach each team member to apply and develop their strengths.

Here are the steps to building a strengths-based culture:

- **Encourage every employee to discover their strengths.** Strengths measurement gives teams a common language to talk about how they can collaborate and perform effectively. Awareness is just the beginning. A strengths-based measurement approach is designed primarily to improve constructive communication and development.

- **Build an internal network of Gallup-Certified Strengths Coaches.** Expert-level strengths coaches serve as internal consultants who can advise managers, give them practical insights and tools, and provide

ongoing support. To meet the demands of the
new hybrid workplace, require your managers to
become Gallup-certified.

- **Integrate strengths into performance management.** To
ensure that strengths become a vital part of your ongoing
business operations, rather than a side program, your
managers need to become strengths-based performance
coaches for their teams. They must first understand their
own strengths and how they can use them. Next, they
need to understand their employees' strengths so they
can have effective ongoing conversations that lead to
performance and competency development. Ultimately,
you will achieve your highest performance when every
member of every team knows everyone's strengths.

- **Transform your learning programs.** Conduct a thorough
audit of your learning programs and practices —
recruiting, hiring, onboarding and the entire employee
life cycle. Identify any programs that wear down your
workforce by contradicting a culture that leads with
strengths. Identifying weaknesses is important, and
everyone will have tasks and responsibilities that don't
perfectly align with their strengths. But to develop
competencies effectively, it is important to first understand
who each person is and what their natural tendencies are.

- **Build a system for selecting all employees into roles
that fit their innate talents.** (See Appendix.) While it's
important for your selection system to fit every employee
to their role, the most essential role to get right in a
strengths-based culture is the manager. Everyone in your
organization has a different work-life situation. You need
managers who are well-positioned to coach each person

they manage using clear goals, ongoing meaningful conversations and accountability. Historically, managers have gotten their roles because of two factors: tenure in the organization and/or success in a prior nonmanager job. Unfortunately, these two criteria are unrelated to the ability to coach employees. The best way to position managers for success is to build a process for identifying their potential.

A robust manager selection system should include a review of candidates' prior experiences, achievements and innate tendencies; multiple interviews; and on-the-job observations of team leading and collaboration. Gallup researchers have spent five decades asking questions, studying responses and tracking the performance of individuals in hundreds of jobs across more than 2,000 clients. We have also reviewed over 100 years of published selection research.

Our scientists have discovered five innate traits, or human tendencies, that predict performance for managers:

- **Motivation:** inspiring teams to do exceptional work
- **Workstyle:** setting goals and arranging resources for the team to excel
- **Initiation:** influencing others to act; pushing through adversity and resistance
- **Collaboration:** building committed teams with deep bonds
- **Thought process:** taking an analytical approach to strategy and decision-making

Gallup has worked with thousands of organizations to implement a system to improve the decision-making process for who becomes manager. An equally important element is rewarding and recognizing vital individual contributor roles so that not everyone feels the need to aspire to become a manager or "move up" the career ladder in the organization.

- **Clarify where strengths fit into your strategy.** If you want a respected strengths-based culture, senior leaders — especially CEOs — need to clearly articulate how strengths fit into the organization's purpose and performance objectives. Here is how two successful global organizations integrate strengths science into their business objectives to increase effectiveness:

  In 2015, global professional services consulting giant Accenture was looking to change its performance management system to something more efficient and meaningful than filling out annual review forms. The goal was to focus on forward-looking performance conversations, instead of documenting the past. Strengths fit into a different and more effective way to have ongoing performance conversations among team members, many of whom can work on a variety of teams during any year. Strengths are aimed at priority setting, giving ongoing feedback and development. A large portion of Accenture's 700,000+ employees have now learned their strengths.

  With approximately 51,000 employees, the multinational medical technology company Stryker has established thoughtful processes around talent-based hiring and strengths-based development to achieve its mission of making healthcare better. Stryker's successful "talent offense" leverages employees' strengths around the world. An essential part of Stryker's global culture and the company's approach to hiring, engaging and developing talent is about respecting people's strengths.

In fact, a strengths-based philosophy has been integrated into a wide range of human resources practices across the company, including acquisitions and talent integrations. This viewpoint helps employees understand each other's unique abilities, ensures people feel seen and valued, and fosters effective collaboration.

For decades, Stryker has been on the cutting edge of talent-based behavioral economics to empower leaders to hire and develop great people that differentiates the company from its competition. Hiring and nurturing the right employees goes beyond strengthening the company's culture and mission. A purposeful talent offense has positioned Stryker for consistently high performance as seen by impressive year-over-year growth. By celebrating employees' strengths, Stryker continues to advance innovations and achieve measurable results while caring for and investing in a diverse global workforce.

Building a strengths-based future

Approximately 500,000 first-year students in hundreds of American colleges such as Furman University, Georgia State University, Kansas State University, University of Nebraska College of Business, Purdue University, University of Tennessee, Villanova University and Virginia Tech learn their strengths and get quality feedback every fall. Strengths is a language that millennial and Gen Z employees or your future employees are already familiar with and expect. These universities are helping turn the U.S. into a strengths-based nation.

PART 4
70% Manager

CHAPTER 27
The Manager Breakthrough

The most important factor in building a winning team is the manager. While Gallup made this discovery decades ago, it is even more important in the new hybrid world of work. Managers account for 70% of the variance in team engagement.

Great managers:

- learn the strengths of each member of their team
- develop and position team members
- make tough decisions about who can best perform each role as the team evolves and grows
- are more likely to attract top performers and retain them longer
- build positive connections throughout the rest of the organization
- cultivate team performance using Gallup's 12 engagement items

The best managers and team leaders also establish trust in leadership. Earlier, we discussed the troubling downward trend in the percentage of employees who feel that their organization cares about their wellbeing. This deterioration is mostly driven by the lack of trust employees have in senior leadership.

Only 21% of employees strongly agree that they trust the leadership of their organization.

In the age of social media, what happens in your organization spreads like wildfire, and this affects your employment brand and your organization's ability to attract stars. Who wants to spend their career at a company with top executives they don't trust? And who really believes that mission statements, visions or organizational values are authentic if they can't count on leaders to do the right thing?

Managers account for 70% of the variance in team engagement.

The big question is: *What causes people to trust leaders in the first place?*

Gallup's workplace analytics team dug deep into our database of 5 million teams and found that the range in how organizational leaders are perceived by teams *within* the average organization was nearly as wide as the range *across all organizations*. Even though teams within organizations have the same corporate leadership, those teams see those leaders very differently. Same company, vastly different perceptions.

No common culture

A major challenge for senior leaders of large organizations is that there is no common culture — even in prominent, highly regarded firms. This is true regardless of those organizations' lofty mission statements crafted to unite all employees toward a common purpose.

Most of the differences in perceptions of organizational leaders across teams in the same organization are based on how each team views its front-line manager.

Of course, senior executives' consistency, clarity and ethics play a big role. But in large organizations, top leaders have minimal direct influence on individual employees. Typically, employees are far removed from the company's CEO and executive team.

When Gallup asked U.S. employees to provide words or phrases that describe their organization's culture, *engaged* employees used words like *friendly*, *supportive*, *collaborative* and *integrity*. *Disengaged* employees used words like *lazy*, *disorganized* and *slow*.

As Gallup highlighted in our book *It's the Manager*, a leader's success depends on their reputation extending far beyond their inner circle. There is a ripple effect in organizations: The reputation of your leadership is filtered through your managers — and your employees' relationships with them.

This is why an organization's highest priority is to make sure its managers themselves are engaged. When managers are engaged, their teams are substantially more likely to be engaged. (See Appendix.) Disturbingly, only one in three managers are engaged in their work.

In short, there is no common culture in most organizations, but *there can be* when organizations make identifying and developing great managers their highest priority.

CHAPTER 28
One Meaningful Conversation With Each Employee per Week

Earlier, we highlighted our finding that when remote-ready employees in collaborative jobs work on-site two to three days per week, they are more engaged and have higher wellbeing.

When Gallup dug more deeply into the data, we found a factor that mattered substantially more than the number of days in the office: 80% of employees who said they received *meaningful feedback* in the past week were fully engaged — regardless of how many days they worked in the office.

The boost in engagement from meaningful feedback is 4x the boost from having the right number of days in the office.

But in a recent study, Gallup found that among nearly 15,000 employees, only 16% said that the last conversation with their manager was extremely meaningful.

What counts as meaningful?

Gallup researchers studied the most common characteristics of extremely meaningful and less meaningful conversations. These are the top five characteristics of meaningful conversations in order of importance:

Recognition or appreciation for recent work. Gallup and Workhuman found that only 10% of employees are asked *how* they like to be recognized and appreciated. And only 23% of employees strongly agree that they get the right amount of recognition for the work they do. Those who do are 4x more likely to be engaged.

Collaboration and relationships. In the hybrid workplace, collaboration and relationships are at risk because people are not physically together as often as they used to be. But Gallup has found that the correlations between coworker relationships and intentions to stay as well as likelihood to recommend the company were stronger in 2022 than before the pandemic. Managers play a key role in connecting the right team partners.

Current goals and priorities at work. Clarity of work expectations has been slipping, especially for younger workers. More remote work means weekly check-ins are essential as customer and business needs change.

The length of the conversation. Between 15 and 30 minutes is enough time for a meaningful conversation, but only if it happens frequently. In fact, 15- to 30-minute conversations have a greater impact than 30- to 60-minute conversations if they occur regularly. But if managers don't give employees feedback every week, they will need longer conversations to catch up.

Employee strengths or the things they do well. Managers can have much more meaningful discussions about how each person gets their work done if those conversations are based on what they do best. The goal of Gallup's CliftonStrengths assessment is to create more effective conversations that maximize the potential of every team member. (See Part 3.)

The takeaway is that feedback is meaningful to employees when their managers focus on recognition, collaboration, goals and priorities, and strengths. And if these conversations happen every week, they can be brief. Naturally, problems and challenges will arise — and managers and employees should discuss them — but to improve engagement, managers need to have conversations that *inspire* each individual.

The one conversation topic that employees perceived as *less meaningful* was discussing their weaknesses or things they don't do well. This might be because, in many conversations, employee weaknesses were *all* that managers discussed. Without the high-priority focus areas above, it's extremely hard for managers to build trust and inspiration.

CHAPTER 29
How to Make Meaningful Conversations a Weekly Habit

So how do you get your managers to have the meaningful conversations that are so essential to employee engagement, especially in a hybrid environment? Managers already have a lot on their plates without being asked to take on another task.

Most managers' jobs are nearly impossible because they have so many new and different initiatives coming at them from senior leadership. Instead of presenting meaningful conversations as just another expectation for stressed-out managers, invest in their development by upskilling them to coach with their strengths.

Gallup has experimented with many manager interventions over the years. Here are some methods that we know work:

1. **Implement strengths-based management.** Strengths-based managing simplifies and streamlines the manager's role. When managers act as coaches for their team, they get progressively better at three things: clarifying the goals of each person on the team, having ongoing conversations and building accountability.

2. **Teach simple science-based insights.** Managers need a straightforward way to understand what works — what leads to big gains — especially in customer outcomes. They need robust insights about human nature that they can count on.

3. **Create learning modules that build on the fundamentals.** In these additional modules, you can expand and elaborate on strengths, engagement and performance development — for example, diversity, equity and inclusion insights or wellbeing insights. Or you can offer hands-on experiences where managers practice check-ins with employees.

4. **Encourage coaching conversations with strengths experts.** Many managers benefit greatly from getting feedback from experienced certified strengths coaches — on their strengths and on their learning strategies for how to maximize the strengths of their team.

5. **Support peer learning.** Managers can get valuable insights and see what ownership looks like when other managers describe their challenges, ideas and successes.

How does Gallup know this works?

Following the onset of COVID-19, Gallup conducted 17 studies on the effectiveness of the type of upskilling described above. In each study, we had a test group of managers who went through a strengths-based coaching manager developmental program and control groups who didn't. The studies included 14,774 participants and 2,354 teams.

Gallup measured managers' engagement, their teams' engagement, their teams' turnover rates and their productivity a year before they participated in the program — and then again nine to 18 months after they had completed the core modules of the program.

We found that managers in the upskilled group had 10% to 22% higher engagement themselves, 8% to 18% higher team engagement, 21% to 28% lower turnover and 20% to 28% higher likelihood of performance improvement relative to their peers. Plus, these effects compound in future years.

Once your managers get into the habit of having meaningful conversations with employees every week, you'll see higher engagement, improved performance and lower turnover. And empowering managers to coach will become an expectation in your organization's culture.

CHAPTER 30
The Hard Job of Managing

> **Managers are handling the most baffling material on Earth: people.**
>
> — *The Economist*

Managers are asked to take on many difficult responsibilities. But no task is more important, especially in the new hybrid workplace, than *having meaningful ongoing conversations with each team member.* Consider how much easier the following demands of managing would be:

- meeting senior leadership's expectations by translating the company's vision
- proactively communicating change to build buy-in among team members
- managing expectations, communication and relationships across stakeholders, teams and divisions
- keeping up to date on the industry, market, business and customers and sharing that knowledge
- gathering input and analyzing information and data to make decisions
- investing in high performers and managing low performers
- motivating high performance
- evaluating team progress

- initiating tough conversations to resolve conflicts
- knowing the hours, technology, budgets, timelines and systems required to get work done while adapting as changes occur
- monitoring timesheets, pay and expenses
- managing diversity, equity and inclusion
- developing star employees
- onboarding, retaining and terminating employees

Each person has different strengths, distinct goals and career ambitions, and unique life situations. And as we noted in Chapter 10, half of U.S. employees prefer to have their work and life clearly separated while the other half wants them blended. The job of managing through all these nuances can become overwhelming, especially when combined with every other challenge in life.

Not surprisingly, managers report higher stress and burnout than those they manage.

It is no wonder that burnout has risen more sharply for midlevel and upper-midlevel managers than for senior leadership or individual employees. These managers are sandwiched between the front office and the front line.

Many managers, no doubt, regret taking the role. Most became managers because they had ambitions to advance in their organization, and promotion was the only route to higher pay and

Managers report **higher stress and burnout** than those they manage.

status. Becoming a manager was a reward and a rite of passage for a loyal employee with tenure.

Teams need great front-line managers who are thriving — not overwhelmed and struggling.

Priority one: Address manager engagement

As we noted earlier, only one in three managers are engaged at work. And fewer than one in 10 managers or leaders have received *training or coaching* on how to manage effectively in a hybrid environment. To win in the new world of work, senior leadership needs to increase manager engagement and certify managers on the skills they desperately need.

Everyone is looking for a silver bullet. Strengths-based management actually *is* one. In the new world of strengths-based management, the engagement of the global workplace could conceivably triple in our lifetimes. Consider the implications of such a dramatic increase on global productivity, customer value and the wellbeing of society. Then consider the alternative.

PART 5
Gallup's CEO Playbook

OUR RECOMMENDATIONS FOR THE NEW WORKPLACE

1 **Commit to hybrid work for your remote-ready employees.** Do this or nobody with any talent will ever work for your firm again. This is your biggest current decision and has extraordinary implications for your revenue growth, earnings and stock price.

2 **Establish Tuesday, Wednesday and Thursday as on-site days.** Don't make this a policy. Announce it as your new way of working — a promise employees make to each other, not a promise they make to management. You need to know which days you are all together for maximum collaboration and innovation. Your customers and suppliers need to know when you're in the office too.

Not all employees will be hybrid, of course. One in 10 of your office and executive workers want to be on-site Monday through Friday, and some will be fully remote. Team leaders need to know each employee's work arrangement so they can manage everyone effectively.

3 **Make sure your managers hold one meaningful conversation per week with each employee.** A weekly 15- to 30-minute conversation about relationships, goals, customers, strengths, wellbeing and recognition can prevent your employees from becoming like gig workers. This one habit develops high-performance relationships more than any other management activity.

4 **Conduct a Gallup culture audit.** This audit is a highly qualitative, thorough review of your current and desired culture. Identify the culture you want. Gallup will evaluate your strengths, weaknesses and opportunities and give you a road map to your highest productivity ever.

5 **Select the right dashboard.** W. Edwards Deming said, "If you do not know how to ask the right question you discover nothing." Throughout this book, we've discussed several important Gallup trends and discoveries. These findings were inspired by our long history of crafting exactly the right questions. Perfectly worded questions create a reliable benchmark of *where you are today* and *where you want to be in the future.*

As we mentioned earlier, there is a new Q^{12} dashboard that aligns with how people work and live today. We call this new dashboard Gallup Q^{12+} because it uses our time-tested insights and adds essential new ones.

Gallup Q^{12+} includes:

Gallup's Q^{12} instrument. The Q^{12} items are the world's most highly validated items for benchmarking a team's progress. The instrument (See Chapter 5) has been tested through 10 iterations of meta-analytics and across wide economic fluctuations.

New items. These items meet the demands of the new will of the workplace:

Respect. Respect is the most basic human requirement at work. Disrespect is toxic. Gallup found that respect is fundamental to making diversity, equity and inclusion efforts work. Every employee in your organization should be able to strongly agree with this statement: "At work, I am treated with respect."

Wellbeing. Prior to the pandemic, millennial and Gen Z workers expected their employers to improve their overall lives and wellbeing, not just provide a job. This expectation has intensified since the pandemic. However, as highlighted in Chapter 15, organizations are failing to meet this expectation. Every single employee should be able to strongly agree with this statement: "My organization cares about my overall wellbeing."

Coaching habit. As we noted above, the most important manager habit for leading the new hybrid and remote workforce is having one meaningful conversation with each employee once a week. Every employee in your organization should be able to strongly agree with this statement: "I have received meaningful feedback in the last week."

Customer. Gallup has conducted meta-analyses of customer perceptions that predict customer retention and business growth. The employee question item most highly correlated with customer retention is: "My organization always delivers on the promise we make to customers."

Your values. If your unique culture requires customized question items, Gallup can help you design your own set of questions that fit into your Q^{12^+}.

6 **Certify all your team leaders as strengths-based managers.** Managers and team leaders are failing at managing hybrid and remote teams. They are as disengaged as the people they lead. They also are experiencing burnout at historic rates. Gallup has packed everything we know about inspiring managers and the new workforce into one developmental program — Gallup-Certified Manager — that transforms your whole organization.

7 **And lastly, aim every hybrid and remote workplace decision at customer retention.**

The workforce has permanently changed and now threatens the very survival of every organization. The risk of employees disconnecting from your organization and becoming more like gig workers is here.

But it doesn't have to be this way.

Your organization *can* achieve historically high productivity. The key to winning the future isn't commanding people back to the office — it's developing strengths-based managers who create an environment where employees experience unimaginable success.

APPENDIX
Gallup Meta-Analyses of Gallup Path Linkages

Gallup meta-analysis researchers:

Jim Asplund, Sangeeta Agrawal,
Stephanie Plowman, Anthony Blue,
Cheryl Fernandez, Frank Schmidt,
Jim Harter

Background

The Gallup Path outlines a definitive set of steps that describe the role human nature plays in business outcomes. This report provides a detailed review of the meta-analytic research that supports each of the major elements of The Gallup Path and demonstrates the practical value of improving the relationships and interactions of leaders, managers, employees and customers. These findings are especially important in the newly evolved workplace with significantly more variance in when and where employees work — bringing increased business challenges for managers and leaders to retain and grow customers, profit and shareholder value.

Meta-analysis

A meta-analysis is a statistical integration of data accumulated across many different studies. As such, it provides uniquely powerful information because it controls for measurement and sampling errors and other idiosyncrasies that distort the results of individual studies. A meta-analysis eliminates biases and provides an estimate of the true relationship between two or more variables. Statistics typically calculated during meta-analyses also allow the researcher to explore the presence, or lack, of moderators of relationships.

More than 1,000 meta-analyses have been conducted in the psychological, educational, behavioral, medical and personnel selection fields. Meta-analysis allows researchers to estimate the mean relationships between variables and make corrections for artifactual sources of variation in findings across studies. This report will not provide a full review of meta-analysis. Rather, the authors encourage readers to consult the following sources for background information and detailed descriptions of the more recent meta-analytic methods: Schmidt and Hunter (2015); Schmidt (1992); Hunter and Schmidt (1990, 2004); Lipsey and Wilson (1993); Bangert-Drowns (1986); and Schmidt et al. (1985).

The goal of any scientific research program is the accumulation of knowledge that can be used to develop and refine theories that explain the phenomena being studied. Since the 1930s, Gallup researchers have been generating research data and studies, and meta-analysis has provided the means of synthesizing this large body of work into robust, practical findings that can be applied in many settings. Since the 1990s, Gallup researchers have published many meta-analyses using methods pioneered by Dr. Jack Hunter and Dr. Frank Schmidt. The studies in this report were conducted using the Hunter-Schmidt methods random effects model meta-analysis (Schmidt & Hunter, 2015), and researchers corrected for artifactual sources of variation such as sampling error, measurement error and range restriction, where possible. For most independent variables, artifact distributions were used to correct for measurement error, and test-retest reliability estimates were used based on Scenario 23 in Schmidt and Hunter (1996).

The unit of analysis for these studies was either the business unit or the individual. In some cases, concurrent validity studies were conducted where independent and dependent variables were measured in roughly the same time period. Where available, predictive validity studies were preferred; these involve measuring independent variable(s) at time 1 and performance at time 2. Studies focusing on strengths interventions were typically quasi-experimental interventions where employees receiving some strengths treatment are compared to control employees who did not receive the treatment.

Analyses included weighted average estimates of true validity; estimates of standard deviation of validities; and corrections made for sampling error, measurement error in the dependent variables, and range variation and restriction in the independent variable. Independent variables were also corrected for measurement error. The most basic form of meta-analysis corrects variance estimates only for sampling error. Other corrections recommended by Hunter and Schmidt (1990, 2004) and Schmidt and Hunter (2015) include correction for measurement and statistical artifacts such as range restriction and measurement error in the performance variables gathered.

While conducting many of these studies, Gallup researchers gathered performance-variable data for multiple time periods to calculate the reliabilities of performance measures. When these multiple measures were not available for a study, researchers used artifact distributions meta-analysis methods (Hunter & Schmidt, 1990, pp. 158-197; Hunter & Schmidt, 2004) to correct for measurement error in the performance variables. The artifact distributions were based on test-retest reliabilities, where they were available, from various studies. The procedure followed for calculation of business/work unit outcome-measure reliabilities was consistent with scenario 23 in Schmidt and Hunter (1996).

It could be argued that, because the independent variables are used in practice to predict outcomes, the practitioner must live with the reliability of the instrument being used. However, correcting for measurement error in the independent variable answers the theoretical question of how the actual constructs relate to each other. Therefore, for most of the meta-analyses, we present analyses both before and after correcting for independent variable reliability.

In correcting for range variation and range restriction, there are fundamental theoretical questions that need to be considered relating to whether such correction is necessary. In personnel selection, validities are routinely corrected for range restriction because in selecting applicants for jobs, those scoring highest on the predictor are typically selected. This results in explicit range restriction that biases observed correlations downward (i.e., attenuation). But in arenas outside personnel selection, one could argue that there is no explicit range restriction because we are studying results as they exist in the workplace. However, we have observed that companies vary in how they encourage employee initiatives and in how they have or have not developed a common set of values and a common culture. Therefore, the standard deviation of the population of individuals/units across organizations studied will be greater than the standard deviation within the typical company. This variation in standard deviations across companies can be thought of as indirect range restriction (as opposed to direct range restriction). Improved indirect range restriction corrections have been incorporated into these meta-analyses (Hunter et al., 2006).

In our research, we used the Schmidt and Le (2004) meta-analysis package (the artifact distribution meta-analysis program with correction for indirect range restriction). The program package is described in Hunter and Schmidt (2004).

For several of The Gallup Path elements, we provide multiple meta-analyses that examine different facets of each path element. For example, the impact of The Path element "Great Manager (70%)" can be studied through the impact of manager upskilling programs, the impact of manager engagement, how managers are perceived by their employees on team employee engagement and the selection of managers. The Path element "Strengths to Role" can be examined through both the efficacy of selection systems and the impact of strengths development interventions. The results of the various meta-analyses contained in this report indicate high generalizability across organizations in the relationships between various Path elements and a diverse set of organizational outcomes — employee and customer engagement, employee turnover, accidents on the job, financial results and so on. Across outcomes, most of the variability in correlations across organizations was the result of sampling error, measurement error or range restriction in individual studies, providing strong evidence of generalizability of the findings across different organizations and geographies.

Utility analysis: practicality of the effects

Because the measures and interventions included in this report have been found to be relatively simple to implement, it is crucial to understand the practical utility of their possible applications.

The research literature includes a great deal of evidence that numerically small or moderate effects often translate into large practical effects (Abelson, 1985; Carver, 1975; Lipsey, 1990; Rosenthal & Rubin, 1982; Sechrest & Yeaton, 1982). Effect sizes referenced in this study are consistent with or above other practical effect sizes referenced in other reviews (Lipsey & Wilson, 1993).

One form of expressing the practical meaning behind the effects from this study is utility analysis (Schmidt & Rauschenberger, 1986). Formulas have been derived for estimating the dollar-value increases in output as a result of improved employee selection. These formulas take into account the size of the effect (correlation), the variability in the outcome being studied and the difference in the independent variable and can be used to estimate differences in performance.

A more intuitive method of displaying the practical value of an effect is that of binomial effect size displays, or BESDs (Rosenthal & Rubin, 1982; Grissom, 1994). BESDs typically depict the success rate of a treatment versus a control group as a percentage above the median on the outcome variable of interest. BESDs have been applied to the results of some of the included studies, while some studies have resorted to utility analysis or other means of showing the practical significance of identified relationships. Because of this variation in methods, each will be addressed in the relevant section below.

The following studies will show that each element of The Gallup Path can be used to improve the health and functioning of the organization. The point of the utility analyses, consistent with the literature that has taken a serious look at utility, is that these relationships provide meaningful practical benefits.

Great Manager (70%)

How did Gallup determine that 70% of the variance in team engagement is explained by the manager?

Hundreds of Gallup studies — and 10 iterations of meta-analysis — show that teams with more engaged employees have lower turnover rates, higher productivity, fewer quality defects, fewer accidents on the job, less absenteeism, higher customer engagement, less shrinkage or theft, higher profitability, and higher wellbeing. These findings demonstrate the value engaged employees bring to their organizations. And in companies with manager-led teams, knowing team-level engagement scores is meaningful. But how much influence does the local manager have on the engagement of local teams?

Gallup's Q^{12} is a formative measure of employee engagement that includes 12 actionable workplace elements with generalizable relationships to the outcomes listed above. The composite of the 12 elements is Gallup's overall measure of employee engagement. Managers are in an optimum position to set the tone for their team's engagement by providing role clarity, feedback on progress, recognition, individual development and accountability — and by initiating social connections among the team. The following is a summary of research that can be considered in quantifying the degree of influence managers have on their team's engagement.

1. Gallup's accumulation of work unit-level data across hundreds of organizations and more than 50 million employees indicates that the standard deviation within a given company across business units and teams is approximately 80% of the standard deviation in the population of all business units or teams across all organizations in the database (Harter et al., 2016). This indicates that engagement is not consistently experienced across teams within organizations. In fact, engagement varies widely in most organizations, suggesting it is not dependent on an overarching organizational culture, but rather, it is highly influenced at the team level.

2. Gallup researchers conducted a longitudinal analysis to test four models of the relationship between executive, manager and front-line engagement across 430 organizations (Agrawal & Harter, 2010). The best-fitting model was one postulating that executive engagement cascades to manager engagement, which then cascades to the front line. That is, the structural model that suggested that executive engagement directly affects both manager and front-line engagement had poor fit to the data, while the model suggesting that executives' engagement affects managers and that managers' engagement affects the front line had excellent fit to the data. Therefore, there is strong evidence that engagement cascades through local management (from executive to manager and from manager to the front line). The path coefficient specifying the relationship between executive and manager engagement (0.55) was equivalent to the path coefficient specifying the relationship between manager and front-line engagement (0.55). Local management's direct influence on front-line engagement is nearly

twice as great as executives' indirect influence on front-line engagement. The percent variance in engagement accounted for in front-line management is three times greater from manager to front-line employee than it is from executive to front-line employee.

3. Q^{12} items with some independent direct effect from senior leadership to the front line were: mission and purpose, knowing what's expected, and progress discussions. Executive leaders are in a position to establish a clear purpose and ongoing priorities and to legislate systems for continuous progress discussions.

4. Gallup researchers have designed a supervisor effectiveness index that has been administered to 52,585 teams in Gallup's client database. The index, including three items with a Cronbach's alpha reliability of 0.96 at the team level, focuses specifically on the employees' perceptions of the manager (active support of organizational changes, creating a trusting and open environment, and inspiring high performance). The observed correlation of the supervisor index with the full Q^{12} is 0.87 after controlling for team size and the number of Q^{12} survey administrations completed. This estimate is uncorrected for the reliability of the measures of supervisor effectiveness and engagement and is therefore a conservative, lower-bound estimate. Based on the observed correlations, employees' perceptions of their supervisor account for approximately 76% of the variance in team-level engagement scores. After correcting for random response error (Cronbach's alpha) in both measures, the correlation is 0.93 and 87% of the variance is explained.

The above findings have been replicated for teams in 11 industries. These findings indicate that the manager accounts for between 69% and 94% of the variance in team engagement.

5. Since there are many possible supervisory influences on team-level engagement, Gallup researchers also considered employee perceptions of organizational leadership as an indicator of team-level engagement.

As noted above, executives influence the engagement of front-line employees primarily through their influence on managers. In addition to employees' perceptions of their manager, the independent effect of senior leadership may also influence the engagement of the team. Gallup's leadership index focuses specifically on the employees' perception of senior leaders (confidence in the company's financial future, leadership makes them enthusiastic about the future and leadership treats them with respect). The leadership index has been administered to 2,329 teams and has a reliability of 0.95 (Cronbach's alpha). This large database enabled researchers to control for the influence of organizational leadership on the relationship between the supervisor effectiveness index (above) and team-level engagement. The partial correlation of the supervisor index with team-level engagement was 0.76 after controlling for team size, number of survey administrations and the leadership index. This estimate is based on observed correlations, uncorrected for measurement error. Correcting for random response error (via Cronbach's alpha for the two measures) results in a partial correlation of 0.91 or the supervisor index accounting for 83% of the variance in team-level engagement, after controlling for the leadership index.

6. In addition to their direct influence on team-level engagement from the perspective of employees (supervisor effectiveness index), managers can also potentially influence team engagement through *their own engagement* and *their own natural traits* or tendencies (talent). Based on the cascade analysis noted above (point 2) and Gallup's meta-analysis of managerial talent (motivation, workstyle, initiation, collaboration and thought process) and team engagement, Gallup compiled a correlation matrix — including the relationship between the supervisor index, leadership index, manager's engagement, manager's natural talent and team engagement. The correlation matrix was used to conduct a multiple regression analysis to assess the combined impact of the team's perceptions of the manager (controlling for team size, number of administrations and leadership index), the manager's own engagement, and the manager's natural talents on the team's engagement. Given the high partial correlation of the supervisor index with team-level engagement, these additional variables, while significantly related to team-level engagement, did not account for substantial additional variance — possibly because they are causal indicators of the perception employees have of their manager. Combined, the multiple correlation was 0.92, indicating the manager can account for as much as 85% of the variance in engagement.

7. To account for other factors beyond leadership that may explain variance in team engagement, researchers considered other database items and indices that are commonly used alongside Gallup's Q^{12} instrument. As indicated above (point 4), after controlling for team size and number of survey administrations, the supervisor effectiveness index accounts for 76% of the variance in team engagement. Perceptions of leadership (leadership index) account for an additional 11% of the variance in team engagement. Other variables that accounted for 2% to 3% of additional variation in team engagement were: perceived cooperation across departments, perceptions that employees trust their company to be fair to everyone and perception that the company cares about their wellbeing. Combined, these variables account for 94% of the variance in team engagement.

Given the variation in estimates generated above, taken from various analytic angles, *conservatively*, it appears managers can account for at least 70% of the variance in team-level employee engagement.

The relationship between manager engagement and employee engagement

Gallup has found that only about one in three managers are engaged in their work and workplace — essentially, the same proportion are engaged as those they manage. Gallup has also reported increasing levels of burnout among managers in recent years. During this same time, employee engagement across the workforce has been declining after a decade of growth. Gallup maintains a large database of organizational employee engagement data spanning more than two decades and including approximately

50 million employee responses to the Gallup Q^{12} instrument across 5 million teams. Theoretically, one of the most important reasons for managers to be engaged in their jobs is that when they feel involved and enthusiastic about their work, it cascades to their teams, resulting in higher performance and better employee retention. Indeed, at the organizational level of analysis, Gallup has found a cascade effect — organizations with more engaged leaders have more engaged managers who then have more engaged individual contributors (Agrawal & Harter, 2010). In this particular study, we studied the relationship between individual manager engagement and their team's engagement across 290,820 manager-led teams in 1,401 organizations for 2019 (pre-pandemic) and 2021 (changed workplace). The goal was to document the extent of the relationship between manager engagement and team engagement and to study whether the correlation was stronger or weaker in the newly changed workforce.

Method

Gallup accumulated team-level data from its Q^{12} client database for 2019 and 2021. Client records or survey questions were used to identify the manager of each team, enabling estimation of the correlation between manager engagement and team engagement across 103,326 teams in 583 organizations in 2019 and 187,494 teams in 818 organizations in 2021. A correlation coefficient was calculated for each company, and then meta-analytic methods were applied to estimate the true score correlation for each year. Artifact distributions were developed to correct for the test-retest reliability of employee engagement across teams and managers. These distributions were taken from previous Gallup Q^{12} meta-analyses. An artifact distribution was also developed to correct for the variation in engagement standard deviations across companies.

Results

TABLE 1

The Relationship Between Manager Engagement and Team Engagement: Meta-Analytic Statistics

Year	N	K	r	SDr	ρ	SDρ	90% CV	% variance accounted for — sampling error	% variance accounted for
2019	103,326	583	0.23	0.09	0.40	0.00	0.40	100.00	103.20
2021	187,494	818	0.25	0.09	0.43	0.06	0.36	48.33	84.52

Source: Gallup

Complete meta-analytic findings are presented in Table 1. The true score correlation estimate was 0.40 in 2019 and 0.43 in 2021. For both years, the correlation between manager and team engagement was of similar magnitude and highly generalizable across organizations. The true score correlation was slightly stronger in 2021, but the data also indicate that there are some slight differences in the correlation across companies. Gallup researchers attempted to identify partial moderators of the relationship between manager and team engagement in 2021. We studied the differences in correlations across different industries and company sizes. There was no discernable difference in correlation for industries with more remote-ready employees. There was a slightly higher correlation between manager and team engagement for those in small companies (less than 100 employees). But the correlations were of similar magnitude for managers and employees in all company sizes.

Practical value

Gallup researchers conducted utility analysis to estimate the practical value on team engagement when improving manager engagement. Based on the meta-analytic observed correlation, managers whose engagement is in the top quartile would have teams that have 11 percentile points higher engagement than average (61st percentile). Managers in the top decile on engagement would have teams that are 15 percentile points higher than average (65th percentile). Based on the true score correlations, managers with top-quartile engagement would have teams with engagement that is 18 percentile points higher than average (68th percentile). Managers in the top engagement decile would have teams with engagement that is 24 percentile points higher than average (74th percentile).

The Impact of Manager Upskilling

The workplace has changed, and the pace of disruption is increasing. Managers must lead differently in the face of new challenges. Today's employees demand meaningful work, managers who care for them as people, ongoing communication, clear work expectations, and opportunities to learn and grow. They want a coach, not a boss.

Great managers consistently engage their teams to meet these new demands and achieve outstanding performance. But not every team is led by a great manager.

Gallup has developed a manager development program known as Boss-to-Coach (BTC) to help any manager become more like the best managers that Gallup has studied. It follows Gallup's leadership framework to help clients optimize employee talent, transform their culture, and boost organizational effectiveness and client outcomes.

Boss-to-Coach participants receive individualized learning, shared experiences and one-on-one coaching. The most general definition of a BTC intervention is when a respondent completes the entire curriculum, returns to work and begins to put what they have learned into practice. It takes time for teams to change processes — and even more time for measurements of those changed processes to accumulate. For this study, the average latency of post-course measurement was nine to 18 months, although there was considerable variability in latency by organization and course cohort.

Gallup researchers accumulated research studies from all BTC clients with sufficient performance data for both study and control populations. All of these studies were quasi-experimental. When possible, variables that were hypothesized to explain possible differences between nonrandomized treatment and control groups were used as statistical controls in analyses (e.g., demographics, baseline engagement, geography, business/work-unit age, trade area market statistics, tenure, job type and product type).

Study organizations came from six industries: software, retail banking, healthcare, logistics, medical device manufacturing and electric utilities. The total study population included individuals and business/work units from six organizations and 32 countries. The included studies all employed one or more of the following dependent variables:

- individual employee engagement (the engagement of the person who completed the BTC course)
- team employee engagement (the engagement of the team(s) managed by the person who completed BTC)
- team employee turnover (the turnover of the team(s) managed by the person who completed BTC)
- individual performance metrics for the BTC participants

Results

Meta-analytic and validity generalization statistics for the relationships are shown in Table 2.

TABLE 2

Meta-Analysis of Relationship Between Outcomes and BTC Intervention

Individual-level analysis	Engagement	Performance
Number of individuals/teams	12,715	13,040
Number of r's	5	2
Mean observed r	0.10	0.24
Observed SDr	0.01	0.01
Mean observed d	0.19	0.51
True effect size r[1]	0.16	0.33
True effect size d[1]	0.32	0.75
% Variance accounted for — sampling error	0	297
% Variance accounted for[1]	100	1,663
90% CVr	0.16	0.33
90% CVd	0.32	0.75
95% Confidence interval lower r	0.14	0.32
95% Confidence interval upper r	0.17	0.35
95% Confidence interval lower d	0.29	0.72
95% Confidence interval upper d	0.35	0.79

Team-level analysis	Engagement	Turnover
Number of individuals/teams	2,354	2,319
Number of r's	6	4
Mean observed r	0.09	-0.16
Observed SDr	0.03	0.02
Mean observed d	0.18	-0.32
True effect size r[1]	0.13	-0.23
True effect size d[1]	0.26	-0.48
% Variance accounted for — sampling error	0	471
% Variance accounted for[1]	284	890
90% CVr	0.13	-0.23
90% CVd	0.26	-0.48
95% Confidence interval lower r	0.09	-0.20
95% Confidence interval upper r	0.16	-0.25
95% Confidence interval lower d	0.18	-0.41
95% Confidence interval upper d	0.33	-0.54

[1] Includes correction for dependent-variable measurement error and correction for unequal sample sizes

r = correlation | SD = standard deviation | CV = credibility value

Source: Gallup

The findings show generalizability across organizations, as indicated by the 90% credibility values, all of which match the direction of the hypothesized relationships. That is, course completion effectively predicts the outcomes in the expected direction across organizations, including those in different industries and different countries.

The sample of studies has much less variance between the effect sizes than would be expected by sampling error. This often happens with small numbers of studies per table entry, as was the case here. As a consequence, the estimated variance attributable to artifacts exceeded the total observed variability.

We generated estimates of utility for all outcomes to simplify interpretation. Estimates are in Table 3.

TABLE 3

Estimated Utility Across Outcomes

Outcome	Estimated utility	
	Low	High
Employee engagement increase (Participant)	10%	22%
Employee engagement increase (Team)	8%	18%
Performance: Increased likelihood of high performance (Represents higher probability of improved performance)	20%	28%
Turnover reduction	21%	28%

Source: Gallup

Conclusions

The intervention in this study was a manager development program. As a group, the managers who completed Gallup's Boss-to-Coach course were successful in improving their post-course engagement and performance more than peer managers who did not participate. The effects of the BTC intervention on business outcomes appear to generalize across organizations.

Strengths to Role

A strengths-based approach to employee development is predicated on the hypothesis that our greatest opportunities for success come from the productive application of individual talents — naturally recurring patterns of thought, feeling or behavior that can be productively applied (Hodges & Asplund, 2009). By refining our talents with skill, knowledge and training, we can develop them into strengths.

In programs designed to promote strengths-based development, feedback is often accompanied by instruction, experiential learning, and mentoring activities designed to help people develop strengths associated with occupational or educational roles. CliftonStrengths results provide a foundation for discussion with managers and colleagues to drive behavioral change. For most businesses, those desired behavioral changes are proximate goals, intended to ultimately result in measurably improved performance. The performance measures of greatest interest to most firms generally include team cohesion and engagement, customer engagement and retention, employee retention, productivity, and financial success.

The most general definition of a Gallup strengths-based intervention is when a respondent completes the CliftonStrengths assessment and is made aware of their top natural talents. In practice, strengths-based interventions vary in objective, type and magnitude. In some cases, respondents are given more advanced coaching and training. And in other cases, they are given basic information such as a book or website description and tutorial. In some organizations, the interventions were designed for managers of teams, while in other organizations, interventions were for individual contributors. The dependent variables for business/work units were also quite different from those measured at the individual level.

Researchers categorized strengths-based interventions into six general types. Individual-level interventions included the following:

1. *An individual completed the CliftonStrengths assessment.* Dependent variables were compared with those who had not completed the CliftonStrengths assessment.

2. *An individual manager completed the CliftonStrengths assessment as part of a manager development course.* Manager dependent variables were compared with other managers who did not take the CliftonStrengths assessment or the developmental course. The individual contributor dependent variables for those directly reporting to the manager were collected and studied in a separate analysis.

Business/work-unit-level analyses included the following:

1. *Business/work units included at least one person who completed the CliftonStrengths assessment.* Dependent variables were compared with business/work units in which no one completed the CliftonStrengths assessment.

2. *The percentage of individuals who completed the CliftonStrengths assessment in a business/work unit was recorded.* In this case, the treatment group independent variable could range from 0% to 100%.

3. *An individual manager completed the CliftonStrengths assessment as part of a manager development course.* Business/work unit dependent variables were compared with those of managers who had not completed the course.

4. *An individual manager completed the CliftonStrengths assessment.* Business/work unit dependent variables were compared with those of managers who did not complete the CliftonStrengths assessment.

Individual-level performance outcomes were:

- Sales
- Customer engagement
- Employee turnover
- Employee citizenship
- Employee engagement
- Performance ratings
- Productivity

Business/work-unit-level outcomes were:

- Sales
- Profit
- Employee turnover
- Employee or patient safety

In an exhaustive review of Gallup's inferential databases, organizations with both strengths data and performance data were accumulated. Researchers limited their scrutiny to organizations with a minimum of 30 complete CliftonStrengths responses, and a few studies had to be removed due to a lack of identifiable contrast groups. In the end, 103 studies were conducted in 45 organizations and included 2.1 million individuals.

Study organizations came from a wide range of industries, including heavy equipment and vehicle manufacturing, medical devices, computers, retail and commercial banking, mass and specialty retail, hospitality, electric utilities, finance and insurance, healthcare, aerospace, food and other agriculture products, oil services, automobile retail, building materials, investment services, education, and consumer products.

The total study population was geographically diverse as well, with individuals and business/work units from 111 countries. The number of countries per study ranged from one to 78. While some countries were included in only one study, 79 countries were represented in more than one study, and 44 countries were represented in three or more studies each.

Results

Meta-analytic and validity generalization statistics for these relationships are shown in Table 4.

TABLE 4

Meta-Analysis of Relationship Between Outcomes and StrengthsFinder Intervention

	Number of individuals	Number of r's	Mean observed r	Observed SDr	Mean observed d	True validity r¹	True validity SD¹	True validity d¹	% Variance acct'd for — sampling error	% Variance acct'd¹	90% CVr	90% CVd
Individual-level analysis												
Citizenship	297,511	3	0.062	0.027	0.12	0.096	0.041	0.19	1.3	5.7	0.044	0.09
Customer	9,554	5	0.059	0.048	0.12	0.098	0.064	0.20	22.3	34.2	0.016	0.03
Performance ratings	374,588	14	0.112	0.055	0.23	0.304	0.046	0.67	1.2	88.4	0.245	0.52
Productivity	103,820	11	0.045	0.027	0.09	0.058	0.028	0.12	15.0	30.2	0.021	0.04
Sales	5,816	10	0.104	0.076	0.21	0.143	0.081	0.29	28.9	39.0	0.040	0.08
Turnover	387,575	11	-0.438	0.026	-1.08	-0.533	0.258	-1.49	0.0	13.7	-0.200	-0.42
Engagement	31,201	20	0.161	0.093	0.33	0.308	0.158	0.68	7.1	7.9	0.105	0.21
Business-unit-level analysis												
Customer	1,345	3	0.053	0.013	0.11	0.107	0.000	0.22	1311.2	1566.2	0.107	0.22
Profit	7,188	9	0.129	0.063	0.26	0.251	0.078	0.54	30.5	55.7	0.151	0.31
Safety	423	3	-0.119	0.101	-0.24	-0.209	0.060	-0.44	68.6	87.9	-0.286	-0.62
Sales	9,438	10	0.082	0.052	0.17	0.150	0.054	0.31	37.9	66.7	0.081	0.16
Turnover	1,581	3	-0.214	0.030	-0.45	-0.478	0.000	-1.24	194.3	541.6	-0.478	-1.24

SD = standard deviation

¹ Includes correction for direct range variation within organizations and dependent-variable measurement error

Source: Gallup

The findings show generalizability across organizations, as indicated by the 90% credibility values, all of which match the direction of the hypothesized relationships. That is, CliftonStrengths completion effectively predicts these outcomes in the expected direction across organizations, including those in different industries and different countries.

For some measures, study artifacts explain most of the variance in correlations. For individual performance ratings, business-unit safety and business-unit sales, at least two-thirds of the variance in correlations is attributable to sampling error, range variation or measurement error. The results for business-unit profit measures were similar, but to a lesser degree; over half of the variability in these correlations is attributable to measurement artifacts.

In the case of business-unit customer and turnover measures, the sample of studies has much less variance between the effect sizes than would be expected by sampling error. This often happens with small numbers of studies per table entry, as was the case here. As a consequence, the estimated variance attributable to artifacts exceeded the total observed variability.

For the remaining study measures — all of them pertaining to individual-level analyses — the variance in effect sizes exceeded what might be expected due to sampling and measurement error. This was largely due to large sample sizes in individual studies. The individual-level turnover studies varied widely in terms of sample size — three studies had over 40,000 cases, whereas four studies had fewer than 500 cases — and the largest study also had by far the largest estimated effect size.

The utility estimates in Table 5 represent effects with appreciable practical significance. Since effect sizes varied depending on whether or not control variables were used, we were conservative in our estimations of practical utility. We produced a range of likely utility estimates based on the 10th percentile (90% credibility value) of true score effects and the mean observed effect size.

TABLE 5

Estimated Utility

	Range based on 90% CV and observed d
Individual-level analysis	
Citizenship	4.3-9.5%
Customer	1.6-9.7%
Performance/Productivity/Sales	8.0-17.9%
Turnover	20.4-73.0%
Engagement	7.2-23.1%
Business-unit-level analysis	
Customer	3.4-6.9%
Profit	14.4-29.4%
Safety	22.9-59.0%
Sales	10.3-19.3%
High turnover	26.0-71.8%
Low turnover	5.8-16.1%

Source: Gallup

Conclusions

These findings are important because they imply that interventions can be developed and used across different organizations with a high level of confidence. The data from the present study show that investing in employee development can provide material and psychological benefits to the organization, its customers and its owners.

As demonstrated in the utility analyses above, the observed effects have important practical implications. These findings are all the more remarkable because they are the results of some fairly straightforward interventions that are quite simple to execute. Most of the study interventions involved employees taking the online CliftonStrengths assessment and reviewing a modest amount of related output. In many cases, the intervention was applied quite broadly — perhaps to thousands of employees — in only a matter of weeks.

The Impact of Talent-Based Hiring Assessments on Performance Outcomes: A Meta-Analysis, 3rd Edition, 2023

Abstract

—

OBJECTIVE

Estimate the relationship between Gallup talent assessments and individual performance outcomes.

—

METHOD

Gallup conducted a meta-analysis of 827 studies on the relationship between Gallup talent assessments and individual and team performance. All 827 studies (171,781 observations) consist of assessments pre- or post-hire, across both structured interview phone and automated (web-based or interactive voice response (IVR)) mediums for a wide variety of roles. Therefore, Gallup researchers were able to estimate both the concurrent and predictive validity of the assessments across different mediums and job types.

RESULTS

Gallup talent assessment scores were associated with a range of positive outcomes across all role types. These validities represent substantial practical utility, if applied consistently as one part of the hiring and promotion decision-making process by organizational leaders. For example, using an in-depth Gallup talent assessment to select the top 25% of manager talent is associated with a 46% improvement in the probability of success on a composite measure of outcomes, 13% higher employee engagement of their team members, 37% better financial results and 18% improvement in productivity.

Using a web-based Gallup talent assessment to select the top 25% of manager talent is associated with a 42% improvement in the probability of success on a composite measure of outcomes, 10% higher employee engagement of their team members, 13% better financial results and 6% improvement in productivity. For sales roles, selecting the top 25% of sales talent relates to a 12% improvement in financial outcomes for both in-depth and web assessment modes. For non-sales individual contributor roles, using an in-depth assessment to select the top 25% of talent relates to 23% improvement in customer loyalty and 10% improvement in productivity metrics. Using a web-based assessment to select the top 25% of talent relates to 8% improvement in customer loyalty and 3% improvement in productivity metrics.

INTERPRETATION

Both in-depth structured talent interviews (via phone) and automated talent assessments (predominantly web-based) result in substantial utility. For most roles and outcomes studied, web-based and in-depth interviews can be used separately or in combination after considering tradeoffs in validity, utility and cost efficiencies. Web-based instruments are more cost-effective and can be used exclusively or at early stages in the selection process to identify candidates with the greatest potential. When it is feasible, web-based assessments can be paired with in-depth phone interviews to provide even more robust indications of potential success in a given role.

—

BACKGROUND

One hundred years of employee selection research have demonstrated that organizations can use reliable and valid methods to improve hiring efficiency and subsequent performance and retention of employees (Schmidt et al., 2016; Sackett et al., 2022). Gallup's review of this body of research concludes that the following criteria, when available, should be taken into consideration in hiring decisions:

- **Prior experiences and achievements.** Collect substantial background information on the candidates, including key experiences that align with job demands, educational achievement and evidence of job knowledge.
- **Innate tendencies.** Assess candidates on the five talent dimensions — motivation, workstyle, initiation, collaboration and thought process. This can be done efficiently and cost effectively through Gallup's structured interviews and web-based assessments.
- **Multiple interviews.** At later stages in the hiring process, have the hiring manager and team members conduct multiple interviews with candidates. Interviews allow

the interviewers to contextualize each candidate's fit
to the role, manager, team and organization. Gallup's
discussion guides are developed to improve the quality of
these conversations. Combining evaluations from several
interviews will substantially reduce the bias caused by a
single-interview approach.

- **On-the-job observation.** When possible, use internships
  and other project-based experiences to gather on-the-job
  performance information on each candidate's individual
  achievement, collaboration and customer value. Collect
  ratings from their supervisors and peers.

We will focus on the second of these criteria — innate
tendencies — which Gallup has measured through structured
interviews (phone) or automated (web-based or IVR) assessments
of talents fitting into five general dimensions that are adjusted to
the role based on extensive studies of job responsibilities within each
role family. The five dimensions are:

1. **Motivation:** drive for achievement
2. **Workstyle:** organizing work for efficient completion
3. **Initiation:** taking action and inspiring others to succeed
4. **Collaboration:** building quality partnerships
5. **Thought Process:** solving problems through assimilation
   of new information

Measurement of these dimensions is accumulated into a total
score for each job candidate, which is used, in part, to decide if the
candidate is a good fit for the role.

We will discuss the instrument development steps in more detail later in this section.

Gallup researchers included research studies from available organizations that met the following criteria:

1. sufficient number of study employees with a talent score and appropriate performance measures

2. adequate quality outcome data, either concurrent (among incumbent employees at approximately the same time as the talent assessment measurement) or predictive (where performance was measured at a reasonable time following the pre-hire measurement of talent)

Three previous talent meta-analyses have been published using a smaller subset of studies that are also contained in this meta-analysis (Schmidt & Rader, 1999; Harter et al., 2004; Yang et al., 2020). Researchers also integrated Gallup data into the 100-year meta-analysis (Schmidt et al., 2016) referenced earlier. This meta-analysis contains substantially more studies and, in particular, those of Gallup web-based assessments, which were more recently developed.

In total, we obtained 988 validity coefficients from studies conducted by Gallup researchers and from clients between 1967 and 2020. A majority of studies were accumulated since the previous meta-analysis in 2004. Since all available studies were included in this meta-analysis — a large majority of which were unpublished — there is no risk of publication bias in the results. This large body of studies includes a wide range of industry types including manufacturing, retail, financial services, insurance, healthcare, professional and amateur sports, schools, hotels, restaurants, trucking, and high tech.

Of the 988 coefficients, some were obtained from the same samples (most commonly from multiple performance criteria from the same respondents). Thus, not all data were statistically independent. To correct for this, researchers followed some basic decision rules. In cases where there were multiple measures for the same criterion variable, researchers averaged the correlation across the studies and used one average estimate for the study sample. Where the construct validity was not clearly superior for one measure, researchers used the average of the correlations for multiple studies. When composite performance measures were used in the study, researchers used composite measures in analyses. Composite measures consisted of the sum of several performance measures, as explained later in this section.

—
METHODS EMPLOYED:

- meta-analytic estimates using artifact distributions, reporting observed and true score effect sizes, standard deviations and generalizability statistics
- correction of effect sizes for range restriction in predictive validity studies since candidates were selected using the assessment scores resulting in attenuated correlations to performance
- a utility analysis to estimate the practical value of the effect size estimates of the various outcomes

The final number of validity studies (independent within criterion type) was 827, with 171,781 observations.

—
STUDY RESULTS CATEGORIES:

JOB TYPE

- Leaders/managers: Individuals in these roles have direct or indirect responsibility for the performance of individuals, teams, business units or an entire organization.
- Sales: Sales professionals are individually responsible for their own performance against sales and growth objectives, capturing new top line revenue for the organization.
- Non-sales individual contributor roles:
  - Skilled/highly skilled: Incumbents in these roles work collaboratively or independently with a high degree of ownership, within and across teams, with a specific set of formal skills and expertise.
  - Semi-skilled: Individuals in these roles primarily support other individuals, programs or functions through acquired expertise.
  - Teachers
  - Students

STUDY TYPE

- Concurrent
  - Studies conducted during the pilot testing phase of an assessment build; items that are selected based on a job analysis are piloted among a sample of role incumbents stratified by performance.

- Items exhibiting the strongest psychometric characteristics (including correlation to total score and performance criteria) are retained for the field instrument.
- The performance evidence gathered in the process of building the assessment provides useful concurrent validation evidence.
- All concurrent estimates are true cross-validation coefficients from full pilot assessments, not fold-back coefficients from the retained items within the same samples (the latter are not considered validity estimates since they are inflated due to the specific item properties in one sample).

- Predictive
  - Studies conducted on assessments developed based on concurrent validity evidence are administered to true job candidates.
  - Items are scored into a composite total score for each candidate.
  - These studies are conducted after the candidate has been hired based on the assessment score as well as other criteria and has been in the role for an appropriate amount of time.

MODE OF ADMINISTRATION

- In-depth structured interviews
  - Assessments are administered over the phone.
  - Items are open-ended and have probing or follow-up questions so candidates can dive into details and/or give examples of their relevant experience.

- Respondents are given either a full point or a zero depending on whether their response was keyed to the predetermined "listen for" (an answer consistent with top performers' answers).
- Gallup talent analysts who conduct these interviews over the phone go through a rigorous training process and are required to meet regular interrater reliability checks.

- Automated assessments (web or IVR)

  - Web-based assessments represent the majority of data in this category.
  - Web assessments require the candidate to log in to a Gallup-protected site where they enter a unique ID number and complete a series of items of varying types, including multiple choice, Likert and yes/no.
  - Respondents are given either a full point, partial credit or a zero depending on the item type and response option selected.
  - An IVR assessment is the same as a web assessment but administered over the phone, requiring respondents to enter responses via a phone keypad.
  - Due to the similarity in item types and psychometric properties of IVR and web-based assessments, the small number of IVR assessments will be subsumed under the web-based assessment umbrella for the purposes of this meta-analysis.
  - Given the large number of web-based assessments (96%) compared with IVR, the subsequent analyses and tables refer to this grouping as "web."

CRITERION TYPES OR OUTCOMES:

- composite measures (overall summary of multiple key performance indicators for the role)
- customer ratings (customer satisfaction, loyalty)
- absenteeism (days absent; reverse scored)
- employee retention (team level)
- employee engagement
- financial measures (sales performance, net income growth)
- performance (supervisor) ratings
- observer non-supervisory ratings (student ratings of teachers, observer ratings — including third-party and peer ratings)
- production records (units sold, annual attainment)
- retention (individual turnover; reverse scored)
- workers' compensation claims (reverse scored)

Table 6 shows the distribution of validity studies by criterion type and study type (predictive and concurrent). The most frequently studied criterion type among predictive validity studies is productivity records, such as units produced or attainment of goals data (143 studies), followed by financial outcomes such as sales and profit. The most frequently studied concurrent criterion consists of measures categorized as observer non-supervisory ratings (105 studies). The second most studied concurrent criterion is performance appraisal scores, categorized as performance ratings — supervisor (supervisory ratings).

TABLE 6

Criterion Types

Outcome	Number of studies Predictive	Number of studies Concurrent	Total number of studies	Number of observations
Composite	19	7	26	2,831
Customer	31	2	33	8,561
Days absent	11		11	3,329
Employee team retention	2	3	5	1,036
Engagement	39	39	78	17,054
Financial	126	16	142	21,992
Observer non-supervisory ratings	96	105	201	54,943
Performance ratings — supervisor	44	66	110	21,502
Productivity	143	10	153	25,976
Individual retention	66		66	14,212
Workers' compensation	2		2	345
Total	**579**	**248**	**827**	**171,781**

Source: Gallup

Table 7 summarizes the number of studies and observations by mode of administration and study type. With an increased usage of web-based assessments since the last meta-analysis (Harter et al., 2004), the database of both predictive and concurrent validity estimates has rapidly increased. However, there is a larger number of in-depth studies (461) compared with web-based studies (366).

TABLE 7

Studies by Mode and Study Type

Study type	Assessment mode	Number of studies	Number of observations
Predictive	In-depth	438	49,836
	Web	141	61,615
Concurrent	In-depth	23	3,587
	Web	225	56,743
Total		827	171,781

Source: Gallup

For this meta-analysis, we corrected for artifactual sources of variation, such as sampling error, measurement error and range restriction, where possible. Measurement error was corrected for in most dependent variables based on artifact distributions obtained for previous Gallup meta-analyses. Observed predictive validities for each study were entered into a database, and artifact distributions were developed to correct for direct range restriction and measurement error artifacts.

Table 8 summarizes the artifact distributions of all the predictor and outcome variables in the study, including reliabilities and range restriction estimates of the predictor.

- **Predictor reliability distribution:** The predictor (independent variable) reliability artifact distribution (mean = 0.82; s = 0.04) was taken from reported test-retest reliabilities of Gallup assessments, including both in-depth interviews and web assessments (Harter, 2003). A prior Schmidt and Rader (1999) study used the predictor reliability distribution from McDaniel et al. (1994) analysis of structured interviews, with a mean of 0.84 (s = 0.15). Because Gallup had since conducted several test-retest studies, we used our own local studies in updating this distribution. For this meta-analysis, no corrections for predictor reliability were made to the mean true validity because, in practice, the actual predictor score is used. Rather, for generalizability analyses, the predictor reliability artifact distributions were used to correct the true validity standard deviation.

- **Dependent variable (outcome) measures and their reliability distributions:** Researchers developed separate reliability distributions for each criterion type, based on available Gallup data and distributions published in the literature.

  - **Composite measures:** Composite measures of performance varied by study. Some were managerial outcomes (business-unit level) that combined financials, employee retention and other ratings such as supervisor or customer ratings. Others were a composite based on sales metrics such as percent of quota achieved and sales volume. We obtained two estimates of the reliability of composite measures of performance (composite of financials, customer ratings, employee retention) from Harter et al. (2002) and Harter et al. (2003). These two reliabilities had a mean of 0.75 (s = 0.04).

  - **Customer ratings:** Customer ratings were aggregated across multiple raters for each observation (for each salesperson or manager). We used an average across items contained in the rating form where available. Harter et al. (2002) reported the test-retest reliability of aggregated work-unit-level customer ratings using scenario 23 from Schmidt and Hunter (1996, p. 219). This distribution has since been updated to include 13 entries (Harter et al., 2020), with a mean of 0.62 (s = 0.19).

- **Absenteeism:** Absenteeism variables were hours or days missed (excluding vacations and holidays) for employee groups with similar potential days worked. Ones et al. (1993) found the test-retest reliability for absenteeism measures to be 0.17 for one month. Using the Spearman-Brown formula to adjust to the specified time interval in each of the 10 studies reporting absenteeism criteria resulted in a mean of 0.68 (s = 0.06).

- **Employee retention:** Retention variables included turnover (reverse scored) and months or years of tenure for employees hired using a Gallup assessment. We could not locate any studies reporting the reliability of tenure or turnover at the individual employee level. Therefore, we entered a value of 1.00 (s = 0) with the knowledge that estimates of predictive validity would be biased downward, since no correction was possible.

- **Employee engagement:** Regardless of the specific measure used, employee engagement was aggregated across the responses of employees who report to each manager. We obtained 39 estimates of the test-retest reliability of team employee engagement using scenario 23 from Schmidt and Hunter (1996, p. 219) previously reported in Harter et al. (2020). These 39 estimates had a mean of 0.72 (s = 0.11).

- **Financial data:** Financial variables included dollar sales, number of new accounts, units sold, percent sales of specified quota (to control for differential opportunity) and commissions. Most studies used sales data as performance criteria. The artifact distribution represented the frequency of each measurement period used. This distribution had a mean of 0.79 (s = 0.11). Financial measures used in this study were individual level for all non-manager/ leader roles; however, team-level artifact distributions were used for manager/leader roles as studied in Harter et al. (2020).

- **Performance ratings — supervisor:** Supervisory performance ratings included ratings used for administrative purposes and those used for research purposes during the pilot stage of assessment development. Rating forms varied. Some ratings were on individual items while others were a composite overall rating or an average across items contained in the rating. When both were provided, the latter was used to increase reliability and content coverage. We used the results from Viswesvaran et al. (1996) in forming an artifact distribution with a mean of 0.52 (s = 0.11).

- **Observer non-supervisory ratings:** Ratings by non-supervisory observers included a variety of types such as observer ratings of loan quality for loan officers, ratings of call quality for teleservice representatives, observer ratings of teaching performance and peer ratings of manager performance. Ratings were performed by one person (not an aggregate across multiple observers) and were most similar to traditional peer ratings. We obtained 18 estimates of the reliability of observer and other (non-supervisory) performance ratings by combining the distribution from Viswesvaran et al. (1996) with Gallup client-obtained data resulting in a mean of 0.61 (s = 0.21).

- **Productivity (performance statistics and production records):** Performance statistics and production records included achievement gain (for students of teachers), commissions for sales jobs and percent of productivity goal achieved. For production records, Hunter et al. (1990) found mean test-retest reliability for one week of 0.55. We recorded the various time intervals used in studies of production records and used the Spearman-Brown formula to estimate the reliability for each time period. Based on time intervals used in studies of production records, we formed an artifact distribution based on the frequency of each time period. This resulted in a mean of 0.97 (s = 0.04).

- **Employee team retention:** The retention of team members (for managers) was the reverse-scored annualized turnover rate for each team. The test-retest reliabilities used scenario 23 from Schmidt and Hunter (1996, p. 219) previously reported in Harter et al. (2020). This distribution contained eight entries with a mean of 0.50 (s = 0.26).

- **Workers' compensation:** This was a record of the dollar amount of workers' compensation claims for each individual. We could not locate any studies reporting the reliability of workers' compensation at the individual employee level. Like the employee retention variable, we entered a value of 1.00 (s = 0), knowing that the reported true validities will be biased downward.

- **Predictor range restriction:** As noted previously, the studies included in this analysis are both concurrent and predictive validity studies. Within the main body of this section, we focus on the predictive validity estimates because they provide the best indicator of the relationship between assessment results and future performance. Additional results can be requested from Gallup. Assessment results are often used by organizations, in part, to make hiring decisions. Direct selection based on the predictor results in direct range restriction. For concurrent validity studies, the range restriction came from the incumbent sample selected based on an evaluation process unknown to Gallup; the range restriction artifact distributions were only applied to the predictive validity studies. Recently, we reviewed 80 Gallup studies where range restriction information was available. This distribution had a mean of 0.75 (s = 0.18).

TABLE 8

Artifact Distributions of Predictor and Outcome Variables

Artifact distributions	Total by criteria		
	Value	Count	SD
I. Predictor reliability	0.82	6	0.04
II. Outcome reliability			
Composite measures	0.75	2	0.04
Customer ratings	0.62	13	0.19
Absenteeism	0.68	10	0.06
Employee engagement	0.72	39	0.11
Financial data	0.79	70	0.11
Performance ratings — supervisor	0.52	41	0.11
Observer non-supervisory ratings	0.61	18	0.21
Productivity	0.97	118	0.04
Employee team retention	0.50	8	0.26
III. Predictor range restriction	0.75	80	0.18

Source: Gallup

Results

Consistent with previous studies, the meta-analytic results outlined in the tables show mean observed correlations and standard deviations, followed by estimated true validities, after correcting for dependent variable measurement error and range restriction. As noted above, the results discussed here are primarily focused on the predictive validities of relevant outcomes for different job types. A more extensive list of outcomes by job type as well as concurrent validity-based results can be requested from Gallup. These results can be viewed as estimating the relationships across individuals within the average organization. The findings show generalizability across organizations, as indicated by the 90% credibility values, most of which match the direction of the hypothesized relationships. That is, talent assessments consistently and effectively predict the outcomes in the expected direction across organizations.

The results include the sample size (N), number of studies (K), sample size-weighted mean observed predictive validity (r), standard deviation of observed r (SDr), residual standard deviation (SDres), true validity (ρ, correcting for measurement error in the dependent variable and range restriction), standard deviation of the true validity (SD) and 90% credibility value (90% CV). The 90% CV indicates the 10th percentile of the distribution of true validities, or the point above which 90% of the true validities fall.

Table 9 shows the predictive meta-analysis results by mode (web and in-depth) for those in leadership or managerial positions. The primary outcomes of interest for managerial roles were composite performance, customer ratings, employee (team) engagement, financial outcomes, supervisory-rated performance, productivity and manager retention.

- Both assessment modes (web and in-depth) were most strongly related to composite performance. For both modes, the mean true validity was in the hypothesized direction for all outcomes studied.
- The in-depth interview assessment mode, as indicated by the positive 90% CVs, was highly generalizable across all outcomes. The web assessment mode was the most generalizable in relationship to employee engagement, financial outcomes and retention. The mean validity across outcomes was substantial for both assessment modes — an average of 0.21 for web and 0.27 for in-depth interviews. The practical value of these findings will be discussed in more detail in the utility analysis section.

TABLE 9

Predictive Meta-Analysis Results by Mode for Leader/Manager Roles

Outcome	Composite performance	Customer ratings	Employee (team) engagement	Financial outcomes	Performance ratings —supervisor	Productivity	Manager retention
Web							
N (# of observations)	387	3,542	4,797	7,870	2,833	2,145	1,650
K (# of studies)	4	8	10	12	16	10	4
r (Weighted r)	0.276	0.151	0.119	0.074	0.104	0.061	0.147
SD	0.273	0.056	0.083	0.060	0.158	0.167	0.035
ρ	0.394	0.270	0.199	0.112	0.194	0.092	0.207
SDρ	0.331	0.000	0.100	0.062	0.248	0.222	0.000
90% CV	-0.030	0.270	0.071	0.032	-0.124	-0.193	0.207

TABLE 9 (CONTINUED)

Outcome	Composite performance	Customer ratings	Employee (team) engagement	Financial outcomes	Performance ratings —supervisor	Productivity	Manager retention
In-depth							
N (# of observations)	583	361	303	891	5,902	1,141	1,965
K (# of studies)	13	4	6	20	28	19	12
r (Weighted r)	0.280	0.044	0.164	0.217	0.170	0.179	0.145
SD	0.110	0.054	0.132	0.203	0.092	0.116	0.040
ρ	0.438	0.081	0.274	0.313	0.325	0.273	0.204
SDρ	0.000	0.000	0.000	0.177	0.081	0.000	0.000
90% CV	0.438	0.081	0.274	0.087	0.221	0.273	0.204

Source: Gallup

Table 10 provides meta-analytic results for sales roles across two outcomes — financial results and productivity measures. For both assessment modes, true validities were in the hypothesized direction across all four outcomes and of similar magnitude across the two modes.

- The web mode demonstrated strong generalizability for financial outcomes and the in-depth interview mode for productivity metrics, as evidenced by positive 90% CVs. The mean true validity across outcomes was 0.13 for the web mode and 0.16 for the in-depth mode.

TABLE 10

Predictive Meta-Analysis Results by Mode for Sales Roles

Outcome	Financial	Productivity
Web		
N (# of observations)	2,238	4,538
K (# of studies)	6	16
r (Weighted r)	0.095	0.076
SD	0.078	0.094
ρ	0.148	0.112
SDρ	0.080	0.099
90% CV	0.044	-0.015
In-depth		
N (# of observations)	6,719	10,160
K (# of studies)	83	79
r (Weighted r)	0.093	0.113
SD	0.160	0.097
ρ	0.142	0.168
SDρ	0.163	0.025
90% CV	-0.067	0.135

Source: Gallup

Table 11 presents the predictive meta-analytic results by mode for non-sales individual contributor roles for two relevant outcomes: customer ratings and productivity measures. These findings show that:

- The true validities were in the hypothesized direction for both outcomes and across both assessment modes.
- The in-depth mode demonstrated high generalizability for both outcomes, as evidenced by positive 90% CVs. The web mode was highly generalizable for customer outcomes. The mean true validity for the in-depth mode was 0.39 across the two outcomes. For the web mode, the mean validity estimate was 0.13. As we will show

in the next section, the practical utility of validities of these magnitudes is substantial. It should be noted that at the time of this publication, there were limited sets of predictive validity web studies for individual contributor roles (three for customer outcomes and five for productivity outcomes). Future studies may provide greater insight into the magnitude of differential validity between the two modes for individual contributor roles. We encourage organizations to conduct local validation studies on individual contributor roles using web assessments.

TABLE 11

Predictive Meta-Analysis Results by Mode for Non-Sales Individual Contributor Roles

Outcome	Customer	Productivity
Web		
N (# of observations)	1,820	3,911
K (# of studies)	3	5
r (Weighted r)	0.080	0.085
SD	0.032	0.091
ρ	0.145	0.122
SDρ	0.000	0.113
90% CV	0.145	-0.024
In-depth		
N (# of observations)	1,369	2,438
K (# of studies)	14	14
r (Weighted r)	0.232	0.270
SD	0.157	0.105
ρ	0.396	0.374
SDρ	0.166	0.063
90% CV	0.183	0.294

Source: Gallup

Summary of Meta-Analytic Findings

Findings reported in this updated meta-analysis continue to show positive relationships between talent and a variety of performance outcomes. Higher manager talent as measured by either in-depth or web assessments is positively associated with composite measures of performance, financial metrics, supervisory ratings, productivity measures and retention metrics. Thus, while there is a difference in the magnitude of the true validity coefficients for web versus in-depth, where in-depth is generally higher, it can be concluded that high talent measured by Gallup assessments is associated with highly engaged teams, better financial performance and high team productivity among other outcomes.

A look at the findings for sales roles shows that talent measured by either in-depth or web assessments is positively associated with financial metrics and productivity measures. The true validity coefficients for in-depth measures of sales talent are generally similar to web measures of talent. For financial metrics, arguably the most salient outcomes for sales roles, the two modes are almost identical, thus showing that both Gallup web and in-depth measures of sales talent are very similarly associated with higher financial outcomes.

Finally, with regards to non-sales individual contributor roles, both modes demonstrated positive validities, but substantially higher validities were obtained for the in-depth mode. This may be because of a limited number of web studies for individual contributor roles. Examining more detailed analysis for more complex non-sales individual contributor roles (i.e., skilled/highly skilled jobs) the validities for web and in-depth modes were higher and of similar magnitude. Further, studying the validity reported in Gallup's Professional Associate Web Assessment technical report (2017) — representing more complex non-sales individual contributor roles — validities are approximately double those reported in Table 11. Overall, in comparing validity data across in-depth and web modes, taking into account the outcomes and job types with the most robust data, the study suggests the in-depth mode achieves approximately 25% higher validity, and thus utility, compared with the web mode. That said, both modes can be used to produce additive validity and hiring efficiencies, as we will discuss below.

COMBINING WEB AND IN-DEPTH ASSESSMENT MODES

In addition to examining the validity for each mode, we also studied the validity for combined web and in-depth modes of talent assessment from available data, presented in Table 12. Specifically, these data included information where the web assessment was administered prior to the corresponding in-depth assessment. This is generally the preferred order since the web assessment is positively correlated with the in-depth assessment and is a more cost-effective option. Essentially, a candidate who applied for a job was first directed to complete an appropriate web assessment for the role. They were then asked to schedule and complete an in-depth (phone) assessment with a trained analyst. In keeping with the role types mentioned previously, we also examined these data based on the three role groups: leaders/managers, sales and non-sales individual contributor roles.

Table 12 shows the combined validity for the relevant outcomes across all role types. Across leader/manager roles, composite measures had the highest correlation with talent (0.47), followed by supervisory performance ratings (0.33) and financial metrics (0.32). Financial metrics and productivity measures had identical combined validities for sales roles at 0.17. Non-sales individual contributor roles showed similar results; both customer ratings and productivity measures had highly similar combined validities.

Combining the two assessment modes results in somewhat higher overall validity than can be obtained with a single mode — and provides potential hiring efficiencies because web-based assessments are more cost-effective than in-depth assessments. We'll next examine the practical value of the meta-analytic true validities.

TABLE 12

Predictive Meta-Analysis Results by Role Type for Combined Modes

Outcome	Web plus in-depth
Leader/Manager roles	
Composite	0.47
Engagement	0.28
Financial	0.32
Performance ratings — supervisor	0.33
Productivity	0.28
Retention	0.23
Sales roles	
Financial	0.17
Productivity	0.17
Non-sales individual contributor roles	
Customer	0.40
Productivity	0.38

Source: Gallup

—

UTILITY ANALYSIS

Effect sizes such as those reported here can be challenging to interpret. Conventions regarding the utilities of relative effect sizes (Cohen, 1988) may not be informative because the practical significance of those effects depends on the costs of improvement on the independent variable and the benefits of changes in the dependent variable. The research literature includes many examples of large, practical benefits shown in studies with numerically moderate effect sizes (Abelson, 1985; Carver, 1975; Lipsey, 1990; Sechrest & Yeaton, 1982). We generated estimates of utility for the most relevant outcomes to each job type to simplify interpretation. The formulas used to calculate utility have been derived for estimating the dollar-value increases in output as a result of improved employee selection. These formulas take into account the size of the effect (correlation), the variability in the outcome being studied and the difference in the independent variable and can be used to estimate differences in performance. Estimates are shown in Table 13.

The table lists the generalized percent of impact, on relevant outcomes, of using Gallup selection instruments. These percent gain estimates have been calculated by job type and relate to two scenarios — one in which the selection ratio is 25% and another in which the selection ratio is 50%. Additionally, we have calculated the additive utility of multimode assessment (web followed by in-depth).

We have used the formula: ΔU perselecteeperyear = Δrxy × sy × zx to obtain the utility estimates.

The standard deviation estimates for all outcomes were derived by compiling estimates across organizations in Gallup's database.

For example, given a 25% selection ratio, we found that the increase in above-average composite performance for managers was 42% for the web mode, 46% for the in-depth mode and 52% for the combined modes. Therefore, there is an additive gain of 13% to 24% by combining modes. Across most outcomes and job types, there is a small to medium non-trivial-sized gain in utility by combining modes. Though, perhaps the greatest value in combining modes is in the potential hiring cost savings using web assessments during early phases of the hiring process.

TABLE 13

Utility by Role Type and Mode

Outcome	Validity			Utility					
				Selecting top 50%			Selecting top 25%		
	Web	In-depth	Web plus in-depth	Web	In-depth	Web plus in-depth	Web	In-depth	Web plus in-depth
Manager/Leader roles									
Composite	0.39	0.44	0.47	26	30	34	42	46	52
Customer ratings	0.27	0.08	0.28	3.89	1.17	4.09	6.18	1.86	6.49
Engagement	0.20	0.27	0.28	6.04	8.33	8.48	9.59	13.23	13.46
Financial	0.11	0.31	0.32	8.40	23.57	24.29	13.34	37.42	38.56
Performance ratings — supervisor	0.19	0.32	0.33	12	20	22	20	32	36
Productivity	0.09	0.27	0.28	3.74	11.15	11.59	5.94	17.70	18.39
Retention	0.21	0.20	0.23	9.45	9.31	10.61	5.95	5.86	6.68
Sales roles									
Financial	0.15	0.14	0.17	7.58	7.27	8.70	12.03	11.54	13.82
Productivity	0.11	0.17	0.17	1.79	2.69	2.77	2.84	4.27	4.39
Non-sales individual contributor roles									
Customer ratings	0.15	0.40	0.40	5.22	14.24	14.54	8.29	22.60	23.09
Productivity	0.12	0.37	0.38	1.94	5.97	6.05	3.09	9.48	9.60

Source: Gallup

—

DISCUSSION

The main purpose of this study was to examine the effect of talent assessments on relevant outcomes.

Talent assessments can be administered to role incumbents during the assessment build (piloting phase) or true candidates after the pilot assessment has been reconfigured. The validity evidence collected during the pilot phase is called concurrent validity, whereas the validity evidence collected from individuals hired based on the developed assessment is called predictive validity. Talent assessments at Gallup, historically, have been administered over the phone (in-depth), online (web) or via a phone keypad (IVR). Due to the similarity in item types and psychometric properties of the web and IVR assessments, they have been grouped together for the purposes of this study. There are different assessments developed for different role types that have also been examined here. The detailed results for concurrent and predictive validity estimates across both modes are available upon request from Gallup. It should be noted that the average predictive validity in comparison to the average concurrent validity across identical roles and outcomes was 5% higher. This means that for studies of incumbent populations, validity estimates are likely understated representations of the true predictive validity. As such, concurrent validity estimates provide conservative estimates of the predictive validity. Concurrent validities are often calculated in instrument development studies because they are easier to obtain since predictive validities require tracking performance for up to one year or more following a talent assessment.

Overall, the outcomes studied in relation to talent assessments show a positive relationship that indicates that these assessments are effective in identifying talent that would be successful in a variety of roles.

These positive relationships can be seen for most outcomes across study types, mode types and role types. Also demonstrated is the practical utility of the variety of assessments used across modes and roles on outcomes; additionally, utility for an approach that includes both web and in-depth assessments has also been demonstrated. An important element in the utility of any applied instrument and improvement process is the extent to which the variable under study can be changed. Our current evidence shows that the use of an employee talent assessment results in an increase in important, relevant, practical outcomes for businesses in proportion to the selection ratio that is used (i.e., more stringent (25%) or more lenient (50%)). Finally, it should be noted that Gallup selection instruments should be seen as one part of an effective selection system that also considers other relevant job criteria.

Employee Engagement

Gallup researchers have published 10 iterations of the Q^{12} business-unit-level meta-analysis. The results summarized here come from the 10th analysis. The development of the Q^{12} was based on more than 30 years of accumulated quantitative and qualitative research. Its reliability, convergent validity and criterion-related validity have been extensively studied. It is an instrument validated through prior psychometric studies as well as practical considerations regarding its usefulness for managers in creating change in the workplace. The Q^{12} is a formative measure of "engagement conditions," each of which is a contributor to engagement through the measure of its causes.

The current standard is to ask each employee (a census survey; median participation rate is 85%) to rate the Q^{12} statements using six response options, from 5 = strongly agree to 1 = strongly disagree. The sixth response option — don't know/does not apply — is unscored. The independent variable in this study is the average measure of employee engagement (the mean of the Q^{12} items) for each business/work unit.

Gallup's current inferential database includes 456 studies conducted as proprietary research for 276 independent organizations. In each Q^{12} study, data were aggregated at the business/work unit level and correlated with the following aggregate business/work unit performance measures:

- customer metrics (referred to as customer engagement)
- profitability
- productivity
- turnover
- safety incidents
- absenteeism
- shrinkage
- patient safety incidents
- quality (defects)
- wellbeing
- organizational citizenship

This meta-analysis includes all available Gallup studies (whether published or unpublished) and has no risk of publication bias.

Table 14 provides a summary of industries included in this meta-analysis. It is evident that there is considerable variation in the industry types represented, as organizations from 54 industries provided studies.

TABLE 14

Summary of Industries

Industry type	Number of organizations	Number of business/work units	Number of respondents
Finance			
Commercial banking	6	3,132	21,435
Credit	2	59	581
Depository	21	16,230	176,430
Insurance	10	7,837	79,464
Mortgage	1	27	985
Nondepository	1	94	2,038
Security	4	797	25,833
Transactions	1	73	1,530
Manufacturing			
Aircraft	1	3,411	37,616
Apparel	1	16	111
Automobiles	1	30	1,453
Building materials	1	8	1,335
Chemicals	1	928	8,203
Computers and electronics	3	239	27,002
Consumer goods	5	289	13,098
Food	7	3,116	91,337
Glass	1	5	1,349
Industrial equipment	1	89	639
Instrument	8	535	5,848
Miscellaneous	4	924	22,481
Paper	2	753	27,025
Pharmaceutical	5	4,103	39,575
Plastics	1	133	938
Printing	2	35	716
Ship building	3	882	134,297
Materials and construction			
Materials and construction	4	1,270	29,932

TABLE 14 (CONTINUED)

Industry type	Number of organizations	Number of business/work units	Number of respondents
Retail			
Automotive	4	261	13,614
Building materials	3	1,158	65,001
Clothes	4	1,055	28,937
Department stores	2	752	6,594
Eating	8	1,296	57,104
Electronics	6	1,483	104,273
Entertainment	1	106	1,051
Food	6	7,101	344,559
Industrial equipment	1	11	484
Miscellaneous	12	4,170	158,264
Pharmaceutical	2	8,288	171,463
Services			
Agricultural	1	7	635
Business	4	1,258	16,162
Education	10	1,259	22,142
Government	7	11,127	213,631
Health	68	14,807	326,483
Hospitality	11	1,241	190,473
Nursing home	2	508	28,768
Personal services	1	424	3,226
Real estate	4	321	7,924
Recreation	2	49	1,969
Social services	4	1,621	28,602
Transportation/Public utilities			
Airlines	1	111	2,293
Communications	7	4,234	46,784
Delivery services	1	639	53,151
Electric, gas and sanitary services	5	3,183	28,887
Nonhazardous waste disposal	1	727	28,600
Trucking	1	100	6,213

TABLE 14 (CONTINUED)

Industry type	Number of organizations	Number of business/work units	Number of respondents
Total			
Finance	46	28,249	308,296
Manufacturing	47	15,496	413,023
Materials and construction	4	1,270	29,932
Retail	49	25,681	951,344
Services	114	32,622	840,015
Transportation/public utilities	16	8,994	165,928
Total	**276**	**112,312**	**2,708,538**

Source: Gallup

Table 15 provides a summary of the business/work unit types included in this meta-analysis. There is considerable variation in the types of business/work units, ranging from stores to plants/mills to departments to schools. Overall, 22 different types of business/work units are represented; the largest number of organizations had studies of workgroups (teams), stores or bank branches. Likewise, workgroups, stores and bank branches have the highest proportional representation of business/work units.

TABLE 15

Summary of Business/Work Unit Types

Business/Work unit type	Number of organizations	Number of business/work units	Number of respondents
Bank branch	20	18,118	196,481
Call center	7	1,240	22,076
Child care center	1	1,562	25,661
Cost center	16	3,675	76,758
Country	1	26	2,618

TABLE 15 (CONTINUED)

Business/Work unit type	Number of organizations	Number of business/work units	Number of respondents
Dealership	7	423	16,940
Department	12	1,553	33,132
Division	3	714	134,703
Facility	2	1,080	55,182
Hospital	7	800	69,028
Hotel	9	846	182,953
Location	14	11,414	269,829
Mall	2	216	3,790
Patient care unit	8	2,825	52,703
Plant/Mill	8	2,106	100,871
Region	2	113	13,520
Restaurant	6	588	34,866
Sales division	6	391	21,722
Sales team	6	420	27,543
School	6	409	10,496
Store	37	24,124	893,781
Workgroup (Team)	96	39,669	463,885
Total	**276**	**112,312**	**2,708,538**

Source: Gallup

For the composite measure of engagement shown in Tables 16a and 16b, the strongest effects were found for wellbeing, patient safety incidents, absenteeism, quality (defects), customer engagement, safety incidents and productivity. Correlations were lower but highly generalizable for profitability, shrinkage, turnover and organizational citizenship.

The productivity variable includes various measures of business/work unit productivity, the majority of which are sales data. Of the two financial variables included in the meta-analysis (sales and profit), engagement is more highly correlated with sales. This is probably because day-to-day employee engagement has a direct impact on customer perceptions, turnover, quality and other variables that relate to sales. In fact, this is what we have found empirically in our causal analyses (Harter et al., 2010). In the case of shrinkage, correlations may be somewhat lower because many factors influence merchandise shrinkage, including theft, attentiveness to inventory and damaged merchandise.

TABLE 16A

Meta-Analysis of Relationship Between Employee Engagement and Business/Work Unit Performance

Positive outcomes

	Customer loyalty/ engagement	Profitability	Productivity	Wellbeing	Organizational citizenship
Number of business/work units	25,391	32,298	53,228	2,651	1,693
Number of r's	107	90	162	12	2
Mean observed r	0.16	0.09	0.13	0.56	0.08
Observed SD	0.09	0.07	0.08	0.04	0.01
True validity[1]	0.20	0.10	0.15	0.57	0.08
True validity SD[1]	0.05	4.00	0.05	0.00	0.00
True validity[2]	0.29	0.15	0.21	0.71	0.12
True validity SD[2]	0.07	0.06	0.06	0.00	0.00
% Variance accounted for — sampling error	50	58	46	114	708
% Variance accounted for[1]	78	73	72	729	995
% Variance accounted for[2]	78	73	72	810	995
90% CV[1]	0.13	0.05	0.09	0.57	0.08
90% CV[2]	0.19	0.08	0.13	0.71	0.12

r = correlation
SD = standard deviation
CV = credibility value
[1] Includes correction for range variation within organizations and dependent-variable measurement error
[2] Includes correction for range restriction across population of business/work units and dependent-variable measurement error

Source: Gallup

TABLE 16B

Meta-Analysis of Relationship Between Employee Engagement and Business/Work Unit Performance

Negative outcomes

	Turnover	Safety incidents	Absenteeism	Shrinkage	Patient safety incidents	Quality (defects)
Number of business/work units	62,815	10,891	24,099	4,514	1,464	4,150
Number of r's	128	59	37	11	10	20
Mean observed r	-0.08	-0.13	-0.27	-0.09	-0.43	-0.20
Observed SD	0.06	0.09	0.13	0.06	0.15	0.11
True validity[1]	-0.12	-0.15	-0.27	-0.09	-0.43	-0.21
True validity SD[1]	0.05	0.03	0.10	0.03	0.08	0.07
True validity[2]	-0.18	-0.21	-0.38	-0.12	-0.56	-0.29
True validity SD[2]	0.07	0.05	0.13	0.05	0.09	0.09
% Variance accounted for — sampling error	49	73	8	60	23	40
% Variance accounted for[1]	73	90	37	74	66	63
% Variance accounted for[2]	73	90	37	74	66	64
90% CV[1]	-0.06	-0.11	-0.14	-0.05	-0.32	-0.12
90% CV[2]	-0.09	-0.16	-0.21	-0.06	-0.44	-0.18

r = correlation

SD = standard deviation

CV = credibility value

[1] Includes correction for range variation within organizations and dependent-variable measurement error

[2] Includes correction for range restriction across population of business/work units and dependent-variable measurement error

Source: Gallup

As in Harter et al. (2002), we calculated the correlation of employee engagement to composite performance. Table 17 provides the correlations and d-values for four analyses: the observed correlations; correction for dependent-variable measurement error; correction for dependent-variable measurement error and range restriction across companies; and correction for dependent-variable measurement error, range restriction and independent-variable measurement error (true score correlation).

As with previous meta-analyses, the effect sizes presented in Table 17 indicate substantial relationships between engagement and composite performance.

TABLE 17

Correlation of Employee Engagement to Composite Business/Work Unit Performance — All Outcomes

Analysis	Correlation of engagement to performance
Observed r	0.30
d	0.63
r corrected for dependent-variable measurement error	0.31
d	0.65
r corrected for dependent-variable measurement error and range restriction across companies	0.41
d	0.90
ρ corrected for dependent-variable measurement error, range restriction and independent-variable measurement error	0.49
δ	1.12

r = correlation
d = difference in standard deviation units
ρ = true score correlation
δ = true score difference in standard deviation units

Source: Gallup

Business/work units in the top half on engagement within companies have 0.65 standard deviation units' higher composite performance compared with those in the bottom half on engagement. Across companies, business/work units in the top half on engagement have 0.90 standard deviation units' higher composite performance compared with those in the bottom half on engagement. After correcting for all available study artifacts, business/work units in the top half on employee engagement have 1.12 standard deviation units' higher composite performance compared with those in the bottom half on engagement. This is the true score effect expected over time across all business/work units.

As alluded to, some outcomes are the direct consequence of employee engagement (customer engagement, turnover, safety, absenteeism, shrinkage and quality [defects]), and other outcomes are more of a downstream result of intermediary outcomes (sales and profit). For this reason, we have also calculated the composite correlation to more direct outcomes. Table 18 again indicates a substantial relationship between engagement and composite performance. Observed correlations and d-values are of the same magnitude as those reported in Table 17.

TABLE 18

Correlation of Employee Engagement to Composite Business/Work Unit Performance — Direct Outcomes

Customer loyalty/engagement, turnover, safety, absenteeism, shrinkage, quality (defects)

Analysis	Correlation of engagement to performance
Observed r	0.29
d	0.61
r corrected for dependent-variable measurement error	0.31
d	0.65
r corrected for dependent-variable measurement error and range restriction across companies	0.41
d	0.90
ρ corrected for dependent-variable measurement error, range restriction and independent-variable measurement error	0.49
δ	1.12

r = correlation
d = difference in standard deviation units
ρ = true score correlation
δ = true score difference in standard deviation units

Source: Gallup

Table 19 shows the percentage of business/work units above the median on composite performance for high- and low-scoring business/work units on the employee engagement (Q^{12}) composite measure. One can see from Table 19 that there are meaningful differences between the top and bottom halves. The top half is defined as the average of business/work units scoring in the higher 50% on the Q^{12}, and business/work units scoring in the lower 50% constitute the bottom half. It is clear from Table 19 that management would learn a great deal more about success if it studied what was going on in top-half business/work units rather than bottom-half units.

TABLE 19

BESDs for Employee Engagement and Outcomes

% Above median composite performance (total)

Employee engagement	Business/Work units within company	Business/Work units across companies
Top half	66	71
Bottom half	34	29

% Above median composite performance (direct outcomes)

Employee engagement	Business/Work units within company	Business/Work units across companies
Top half	66	71
Bottom half	34	29

Source: Gallup

To illustrate this further, Table 20 shows the probability of above-average performance for various levels of employee engagement. Business/work units at the highest level of employee engagement across all business/work units in Gallup's database have an 83% chance of having high (above average) composite performance. This compares with a 17% chance for those with the lowest level of employee engagement. So, it is possible to achieve high performance without high employee engagement, but the odds are substantially lower (in fact, nearly five times as low).

TABLE 20

Percentage of Business/Work Units Above the Company Median on Composite Performance for Different Employee Engagement Percentiles

Customer loyalty/engagement, profitability, productivity, turnover, safety, absenteeism, shrinkage, quality (defects)

Employee engagement percentile	Percentage above company median
Above 99th	83
95th	75
90th	70
80th	63
70th	58
60th	54
50th	50
40th	46
30th	42
20th	37
10th	30
5th	25
Below 1st	17

Source: Gallup

Gallup researchers recently conducted utility analysis across multiple organizations with similar outcome metric types (an update of analyses presented in Harter et al., 2002, p. 275, Table 6). Comparing top-quartile with bottom-quartile engagement, business/work units resulted in median percent differences of:

- 10% in customer engagement
- 23% in profitability
- 18% in productivity (sales)
- 14% in productivity (production records and evaluations)
- 18% in turnover for high-turnover organizations (those with more than 40% annualized turnover)
- 43% in turnover for low-turnover organizations (those with 40% or lower annualized turnover)
- 64% in safety incidents (accidents)
- 81% in absenteeism
- 28% in shrinkage (theft)
- 58% in patient safety incidents (mortality and falls)
- 41% in quality (defects)
- 66% in wellbeing (thriving employees)
- 13% in organizational citizenship (participation)

—

CONCLUSIONS

Findings reported in this updated meta-analysis continue to provide large-scale cross-validation to prior meta-analyses conducted on the Q^{12} instrument. As we demonstrated in the utility analyses presented here and in other iterations of this analysis, the size of the effects observed has important practical implications, particularly given that engagement, as measured here, is quite changeable.

Customer Engagement

Customers are vital to any organization, and almost all organizations use some metrics to understand how their customers think and behave toward their brands and products. The primary purpose of these various metrics is to accurately gauge customer attitudes, with the implicit assumption that improvement on the metrics will lead to better business outcomes. Fleming and Asplund (2007) found that wide variability exists in customer perceptions across business units within the organizations they studied. The magnitude of that variance is itself a crucial measure of organizational health. The existence of a broad range of performance variability within a company suggests that the only way to manage that variability and improve local performance is to provide customer feedback at the business-unit level, where it originates. Further, business-unit managers are in the best position to act on the results of the customers they directly serve. Hence, examination of the linkage between customer metrics and business outcomes at the business-unit level is important, both theoretically and practically.

Independent variables

To date, Gallup researchers have conducted two large customer engagement meta-analyses:

1. A business-to-business (B2B) meta-analysis of 23 research studies across six industries and two countries. In total, this study included 108,989 respondents from 19,093 business units.

2. A business-to-consumer (B2C) meta-analysis of 24,059 business units from 35 studies across nine industries and 12 countries.

The measures of customer engagement (CE) used in these two studies differed slightly. In the B2B meta-analysis, CE was measured using 11 items, whereas in the B2C studies, CE was measured using only three of those 11 items. In designing the CE items, researchers considered the emotional attachment element of human behavior. All 11 items used a 5-point Likert scale with a sixth response option ("Don't know/Does not apply") that was unscored.

In each CE meta-analysis, the independent variable was a composite score of all items used. The shorter three-item measure used in the B2C studies was designed to be a shorter version of the full 11-item measure and should be considered broadly equivalent in terms of its measurement of overall customer engagement.

Dependent variables — B2B

This meta-analysis included all available studies in Gallup's B2B customer engagement database, whether published or unpublished, and therefore had no risk of publication bias. Twenty-three studies were conducted in independent companies across six major industries. The business-unit-level outcomes were profitability, revenue/sales, share of wallet, customer attrition, brand preference and days sales outstanding. Table 21 presents the number of companies, business units and respondents represented in each industry. There was considerable variation in the types of industries represented.

TABLE 21

Summary of Studies by Industry

Industry type	Number of organizations	Number of business units/ projects	Number of respondents
Business banking	1 client, 3 panel studies	7,640	93,770
Medical devices	2 clients	4,952	4,952
Industrial supply	2 clients	5,263	5,263
Hospitality	2 clients	769	3,603
Food supply	1 client	24	272
Professional services	1 client	445	1,129

Source: Gallup

Studies for the current meta-analysis were selected so that each organization is represented once in each analysis. For several organizations, multiple studies were conducted. To include the best possible information for each organization represented in the study, some basic rules were used. If two concurrent studies were conducted for the same client (where customer engagement and outcome data were collected concurrently — i.e., in the same year), then a composite of effect sizes across the multiple studies was calculated and entered as the value for that organization. If an organization had a concurrent and a predictive study (where customer engagement data were collected in Year 1 and outcomes were tracked in Year 2), then the effect sizes from the predictive study were entered.

Results — B2B

Tables 22a and 22b provide meta-analytic and validity generalization statistics, and the results show high generalizability across organizations in the relationship between customer engagement and the performance outcomes measured.

TABLE 22A

Meta-Analysis Results of Relationship Between Customer Engagement and Business-Unit-Level Performance

Range restriction (between companies)

	Profitability	Revenue/Sales	Share of wallet	Brand preference	DSO	Attrition
Number of business units	916	9,310	4,690	5,569	615	4,751
Number of r's	4	16	3	10	2	3
Mean observed r	0.07	0.21	0.31	0.45	-0.06	-0.23
Observed SD	0.06	0.16	0.01	0.07	0.02	0.02
True validity	0.21	0.51	0.65	0.79	-0.16	-0.68
True validity SD	0.00	0.19	0.00	0.00	0.00	0.00
% Variance accounted for — sampling error	106	6	269	22	948	113
% Variance attributable to all statistical artifacts	163	62	11,895	627	1,462	3,038
90% CV	0.21	0.27	0.65	0.79	-0.16	-0.68
.ρ (true score correlation)	0.24	0.58	0.74	0.90	-0.18	-0.78
SD of ρ	0.00	0.22	0.00	0.00	0.00	0.00

r = correlation

SD = standard deviation

CV = credibility value

For the quantitative analysis in this study, CE[11] mean score has been used to calculate the performance gaps between top- and bottom-quartile business units. As Gallup has advanced its science, we recommend that clients use CE[3] moving forward. CE[3] measures and manages the same construct of customer engagement with greater efficiency and simplicity. The Pearson correlation between mean scores of CE[11] and CE[3] is 0.95 in B2B context. This almost perfect linear correlation between CE[11] and CE[3] ensures the results of the quantitative analysis using CE[3] will be very close to the results presented here using CE[11].

Source: Gallup

Appendix

TABLE 22B

Meta-Analysis Results of Relationship Between Customer Engagement and Business-Unit-Level Performance

Range variation (within companies)

	Profitability	Revenue/Sales	Share of wallet	Brand preference	DSO	Attrition
Number of business units	916	9,310	4,690	5,569	615	4,751
Number of r's	4	16	3	10	2	3
Mean observed r	0.07	0.21	0.31	0.45	-0.06	-0.23
Observed SD	0.06	0.16	0.01	0.07	0.02	0.02
True validity	0.06	0.20	0.27	0.41	-0.05	-0.29
True validity SD	0.00	0.09	0.00	0.00	0.00	0.00
% Variance accounted for — sampling error	106	6	269	22	948	113
% Variance attributable to all statistical artifacts	169	70	13,474	681	1,548	51,667
90% CV	0.06	0.15	0.27	0.41	-0.05	-0.29
ρ (true score correlation)	0.10	0.33	0.44	0.67	-0.08	-0.48
SD of ρ	0.00	0.14	0.00	0.00	0.00	0.00

r = correlation
SD = standard deviation
CV = credibility value
For the quantitative analysis in this study, CE[11] mean score has been used to calculate the performance gaps between top- and bottom-quartile business units. As Gallup has advanced its science, we recommend that clients use CE[3] moving forward. CE[3] measures and manages the same construct of customer engagement with greater efficiency and simplicity. The Pearson correlation between mean scores of CE[11] and CE[3] is 0.95 in B2B context. This almost perfect linear correlation between CE[11] and CE[3] ensures the results of the quantitative analysis using CE[3] will be very close to the results presented here using CE[11].

Source: Gallup

The strongest effects were found for brand preference, share of wallet and customer attrition. These are self-reported outcomes from the same survey environment in which the respondent was asked the customer engagement items. Therefore, self-reported outcomes are more likely to produce inflated estimates due to mono-method bias.

The correlation between engagement and revenue/sales is stronger than the correlation between engagement and profitability. Revenue/sales is the direct consequence of customer engagement, while profitability is a downstream result of the intermediary outcome (i.e., revenue/sales) and includes additional factors such as expenses.

Comparing top-quartile-engagement business units/projects with those in the bottom quartile resulted in median percentage differences of:

- 34% in profitability
- 50% in revenue/sales
- 55% in share of wallet
- 33% in brand preference
- -63% in customer attrition
- -32% in days sales outstanding

One can see that the above relationships are nontrivial. The relationship between B2B customer engagement and organizational outcomes, even conservatively expressed, is meaningful from a practical perspective.

Dependent variables — B2C

This meta-analysis includes all available studies from 2005 to 2014, whether published or unpublished, and therefore has no risk of publication bias. Thirty-five studies were conducted in independent companies and broad customer-based panel studies across nine major industries and 12 markets. The business-unit-level outcomes were revenue/sales, profitability, share of wallet, customer attrition, brand preference and consumer wellbeing. Table 23 presents the number of companies, business units and respondents represented in each industry. There was considerable variation in the type of industry represented. The majority of these companies are multinational corporations that enabled the inclusion of customer data from various countries and markets, including the U.S., Canada, Thailand, Singapore, Indonesia, India, Pakistan, United Arab Emirates, the U.K., New Zealand, Hong Kong and Taiwan.

TABLE 23

Summary of Studies by Industry

Industry	Number of organizations	Number of business units	Number of respondents
Financial services: Retail banking	8 clients, 1 panel study	12,522	337,132
Financial services: Insurance	1 client, 1 panel study	3,895	21,925
Lodging: Hotels	3 clients, 1 panel study	1,067	55,835
Retail: Grocery	2 clients	2,321	69,630
Retail: Pharmacy	1 client, 1 panel study	118	34,998
Retail: Health/Personal care/Beauty	2 clients	2,054	61,620
Automotive: Maker and dealership	1 client	1,117	27,925
Telecommunications: Cellular	1 client, 1 panel study	956	40,870
Transportation: Airlines	1 panel study	9	5,042

Summary of organizations sorted by industry. There is considerable variation in the industry types represented, as organizations from nine industries provided studies.

Source: Gallup

As with the B2B analyses, studies for the current meta-analysis were selected so that each organization is represented once in each analysis, and predictive studies were preferred where available.

Results

Meta-analytic and validity generalization statistics for the sales relationships are shown in Tables 24a and 24b.

TABLE 24A

Meta-Analysis of Relationship Between Customer Engagement and Business-Unit Performance

Range restriction (between companies)

	Profitability	Revenue/Sales	Consumer attrition (Turnover)	Share of wallet	Brand preference	Consumer wellbeing
Number of business units	2,061	18,252	2,154	818	306	1,667
Number of r's	14	21	5	3	2	3
Mean observed r	0.21	0.28	-0.23	0.19	0.32	0.72
Observed SD	0.11	0.14	0.28	0.20	0.15	0.03
True validity	0.26	0.31	-0.29	0.27	0.41	0.77
True validity SD	0.05	0.00	0.19	0.14	0.00	0.00
% Variance accounted for — sampling error	15	27	13	16	23	44
% Variance attributable to all statistical artifacts	118	83	92	59	106	615
90% CV	0.19	0.31	-0.26	0.24	0.41	0.77
ρ (true score correlation)	0.27	0.52	-0.32	0.46	0.54	0.84
SD of ρ	0.08	0.00	0.22	0.19	0.00	0.00

r = correlation
SD = standard deviation
CV = credibility value

Source: Gallup

TABLE 24B

Meta-Analysis of Relationship Between Customer Engagement and Business-Unit Performance

Range variation (within companies)

	Profitability	Revenue/Sales	Consumer attrition (Turnover)	Share of wallet	Brand preference	Consumer wellbeing
Number of business units	2,061	18,252	2,154	818	306	1,667
Number of r's	14	21	5	3	2	3
Mean observed r	0.21	0.28	-0.23	0.19	0.32	0.72
Observed SD	0.11	0.14	0.28	0.20	0.15	0.03
True validity	0.23	0.30	-0.27	0.25	0.37	0.74
True validity SD	0.05	0.00	0.17	0.12	0.00	0.00
% Variance accounted for — sampling error	15	27	13	16	23	44
% Variance attributable to all statistical artifacts	123	81	98	68	131	628
90% CV	0.17	0.30	-0.24	0.21	0.37	0.74
ρ (true score correlation)	0.24	0.49	-0.30	0.41	0.49	0.82
SD of ρ	0.07	0.00	0.19	0.16	0.00	0.00

r = correlation
SD = standard deviation
CV = credibility value

Source: Gallup

The findings show high generalizability across organizations in the relationship between customer engagement and the performance outcomes measured. Most of the variability in correlations across organizations can be attributed to artifacts such as sampling error, range variation and measurement error. The strongest effects were found for brand preference and consumer wellbeing. These two outcomes are self-reported from the same survey environment in which the respondent was asked the customer engagement items. Self-reported outcomes are more likely to produce inflated estimates as a result of mono-method bias.

Comparing business units in the top quartile on customer engagement with those in the bottom quartile resulted in median percentage differences of 22% lower customer attrition, 40% higher revenue/sales, 27% higher profitability, 27% higher share of wallet, 47% more customer preference for the current brand as the first choice for future business and 56% more consumers agreeing that the brand takes care of their wellbeing.

Variance also exists in the utility of customer engagement across different business outcomes. Nevertheless, business units in the top engagement quartile outperform their bottom-quartile counterparts by at least 20% across all key outcomes, suggesting important practical utility associated with high versus low customer engagement.

TABLE 25

Business-Unit-Level Differences on Business Outcome Measures Between Top and Bottom Quartiles of Customer Engagement Mean

Dependent variable	Number of companies	Differences of business outcomes between top and bottom quartiles on customer engagement mean		
		Mean	Median	Standard deviation
Revenue/Sales	20	41%	40%	0.27
Profitability	5	27%	27%	0.21
Customer attrition (Turnover)	4	-22%	-22%	0.10
Share of wallet	4	27%	27%	0.23
Brand preference	2	47%	47%	0.11
Consumer wellbeing	3	56%	56%	0.13

Source: Gallup

With the very conservative estimation of a 20% performance gap across all business metrics, the financial impact on an organization is substantial.

Conclusions

Given the competitive landscape in business, the need to understand the relationships of customer perceptions and opinions to business outcome measures has never been more important. Customer engagement specifically addresses the key role emotion plays in consumer purchasing behaviors. The impact of emotions on judgments, evaluations and decisions has long been important to psychology and consumer behavior. In fact, customer engagement scores were significantly related to neural activity in the emotional areas of the brain (the amygdala, orbitofrontal cortex, temporal pole and anterior cingulate; Pribyl et al., 2004) as well as subsequent spending behavior. The findings from these two meta-analyses further substantiate the notion that customer perceptions are both quantifiable and linked to tangible business outcomes. Therefore, business practitioners should include emotional engagement measures in goal setting, performance monitoring and appraisal, and corrective actions planning.

It is also worth noting that the top 25% of companies we have studied with the highest growth have experienced a significant increase of at least +0.10 on customer engagement mean scores after one year and one standard deviation growth (+0.21) after three or more years. An important element in the utility of any applied instrument and improvement process is the extent to which the variable under study can be changed. Our current evidence is that customer engagement is changeable, varies widely by business unit and organization, and has significant implications for the general health of the business.

HumanSigma

This study examines the relationships of employee engagement and customer engagement to financial performance. Particular attention is paid to the combined effects of employee and customer engagement on revenue/sales.

The hypotheses examined for this meta-analysis are as follows:

1. At the business-unit level, there is a positive and generalizable relationship between:

   - employee engagement (EE) and revenue/sales
   - customer engagement (CE) and revenue/sales

2. The product of EE and CE is more predictive of revenue/sales than is either EE or CE alone.

3. There is an interaction effect between EE and CE, such that the relationship between EE and revenue/sales is dependent on the level of CE.

4. The relationship between HumanSigma and revenue/sales has substantial practical value to business.

In this study, the unit of analysis was the business unit. The mean of results on the Q^{12} items defined the measure of employee engagement, and a weighted mean of results on the CE^{11} items defined the measure of customer engagement. Dependent variables were annual revenue or sales data for each business unit. Within most organizations, business units had differential opportunities for revenue based on local market, competition, size of operation and other factors less controllable by management. To correct for these local biases, companies often produced goals or quotas that each unit could be compared to. Other companies used revenue growth figures (from the prior year). Dependent variables for the 10 studies were as follows:

- sales growth from the prior year (three studies)
- sales variance from quota (three studies)
- actual revenue (two studies)
- sales per employee
- revenue per transaction (one study each)

Each company was represented once in each analysis. The studies were categorized as either concurrent (independent and dependent variables collected during the same calendar year) or predictive (where the independent variable was collected in Year 1 and the dependent variable in Year 2). Seven (51% of business units) studies used concurrent and three (49% of business units) used predictive methodology. Sample sizes were imbalanced across the studies, with three companies representing the majority of business units available for analysis. For this reason, both sample-size-weighted and sample-size-unweighted meta-analysis and validity generalization statistics were used and compared.

Tables 26 and 27 provide summaries of the business units and companies included in the meta-analysis.

TABLE 26

Summary of Studies by Industry

Industry type	Companies	Business units	Employees	Customers
Financial	4	966	22,569	136,592
Manufacturing	2	18	903	2,028
Retail	3	969	42,950	75,588
Services	1	26	650	448
Total	**10**	**1,979**	**67,072**	**214,656**

Source: Gallup

TABLE 27

Summary of Business- or Operational-Unit Types

Business- or Operational-unit type	Companies	Business units	Employees	Customers
Account teams	1	9	125	212
Bank branches	1	793	11,501	45,480
Call centers	1	17	179	17,858
City centers	1	26	650	448
Dealerships	1	25	6,929	2,832
Divisions	1	8	800	200
Regions	1	147	10,764	73,042
Sales teams	1	10	103	1,828
Stores	2	944	36,021	72,756
Total	**10**	**1,979**	**67,072**	**214,656**

Source: Gallup

In addition to calculating meta-analytic statistics for the relationships between employee engagement to revenue and customer engagement to revenue, we conducted meta-analysis of the relationship of the product (EE x CE) to revenue. The meta-analysis of the product was used, in part, to understand the interactive effects of employee and customer engagement (Hypothesis 2). We used hierarchical regression to test for the hypothesized interaction between employee and customer engagement. To conduct the analysis, we performed the following steps:

1. We developed a meta-analytic correlation matrix of employee engagement, customer engagement, their product (EE x CE) and revenue. This matrix was developed both for business units within companies (without correction for range restriction) and business units across companies (with correction for range restriction).

2. We used the meta-analytic correlation matrix to conduct standardized regression analyses, as follows:

   a. We entered the main effects — employee and customer engagement — at step 1 and step 2.

   b. We entered the interaction term (EE x CE) at step 3. Thus, the variance due to the main effects was partialed out, allowing for variance due to the interaction term to be observed (Cohen et al., 2003).

   c. We examined the incremental change in the multiple correlation (ΔR) from the main effects model to the model including the interaction term (relative to the standard error of Multiple R) in assessing the significance of the interaction.

Table 28 provides the meta-analysis statistics for the three variables studied (employee engagement, customer engagement and EE x CE). Both weighted and observed effect sizes indicate positive (and generalizable) relationships between both EE and CE in predicting revenue (Hypothesis 1). The correlation of the product (EE x CE) is more strongly related to revenue than either independent variable alone (the weighted observed effect size is 58% larger) (Hypothesis 2). After correcting for criterion reliability, the mean effect size (ρ_1) is 0.13 for both employee and customer engagement. The correlation of the product to revenue is 0.20 (54% larger). However, after correcting for range restriction (which provides an estimate of the effect size across business units and companies), the correlation of the product (EE x CE) does not surpass that of customer engagement to revenue. This is because the range on CE within the typical company is restricted at a higher level than is employee engagement. This could be due to a customer brand effect somewhat muting the range within companies and thus accentuating it across companies. The values depicted in Table 28 as ρ_1 are the practical effect sizes we would expect within any company. Those depicted as ρ_2 are the theoretical relationships we would expect in business units across companies we have studied thus far.

TABLE 28

Meta-Analysis and Validity Generalization Statistics

Analysis	Employee engagement (EE)	Customer engagement (CE)	EE x CE
N	1,979	1,979	1,979
K	10	10	10
Unweighted observed r	0.18	0.22	0.25
Unweighted observed sd	0.11	0.13	0.11
Weighted observed r	0.12	0.12	0.19
Weighted observed sd	0.04	0.04	0.05
ρ_1	0.13	0.13	0.20
$sd\rho_1$	0.00	0.00	0.00
ρ_2	0.24	0.35	0.32

N = number of business units; K = number of studies
Unweighted observed r = mean observed correlation to revenue
Unweighted observed sd = standard deviation of observed correlations to revenue
Weighted observed r = sample-size-weighted observed correlation to revenue
Weighted observed sd = sample-size-weighted standard deviation of observed correlations to revenue
ρ_1 = sample-size-weighted correlation to revenue, corrected for criterion reliability
$sd\rho_1$ = sample-size-weighted standard deviation corrected for sampling error, criterion reliability and range variability across studies
ρ_2 = sample-size-weighted correlation to revenue, corrected for criterion reliability and range restriction

Source: Gallup

Hierarchical regressions are provided in Table 29 (Hypothesis 3). The upper part of Table 29 provides results for the practical situation of business units within companies, and the lower part of the table presents the same analysis for business units across companies. In each case, there is a substantial incremental gain in each step of the hierarchical regression analysis. Customer engagement adds incremental information to employee engagement (in predicting revenue), and the interaction term (EE x CE) adds to the prediction. In the case of business units within companies, the increase in multiple R is equal to two standard error units' gain, thus likely beyond chance. For business units across companies, CE added greater incremental information, and the interaction term contributed less, relative to the effect of the linear combination of EE and CE.

TABLE 29

Hierarchical Regression Analysis

Business units within company	Multiple R	Δ Multiple R	SE
Employee engagement	0.13		0.02
Customer engagement	0.17	0.04	0.02
Interaction	0.21	0.04	0.02

Business units across companies	Multiple R	Δ Multiple R	SE
Employee engagement	0.24		0.02
Customer engagement	0.40	0.16	0.02
Interaction (EE x CE)	0.45	0.05	0.02

Source: Gallup

Discussion

Gallup researchers have accumulated a substantial body of evidence that attests to the practical value of the independent effects of EE and CE. The HumanSigma statistic is the product of a design process, the intent of which was to encapsulate the measurement of business-unit-level EE and CE performance into a single number that is related to business performance in a meaningful way.

Combining two correlated measures (CE[11] and Q[12]) into a single composite variable presents the opportunity to have a general "management" variable that represents the net HumanSigma performance of a given business unit. Multiple families of functions were modeled against the data available for this study to produce a HumanSigma function that best fits these data. The resulting HumanSigma function is a nonlinear function of EE and CE performance relative to Gallup's respective databases of EE and CE data. The departures from linearity were included (1) to account for observed patterns in existing data, (2) to correctly specify business units with radically different levels of performance on EE and CE, and (3) to make the function more robust with respect to sampling and measurement error.

Regarding sampling and measurement error, it was decided that HumanSigma (HS) would have significantly more practical value if managers could use it without having to maintain constant vigilance with respect to the amount of measurement error in a given business unit's data, which will vary from study to study. Consequently, HumanSigma data are generally discussed in terms of broad levels of performance, referred to as "HumanSigma levels" in this paper. These levels are simply standard-deviation groups on the HumanSigma function; with six standard deviations of range in the observed data, there are thus six HumanSigma levels, denoted as HS1, HS2 and so forth.

Calculating the HumanSigma levels for the business units in this study, we find substantial practical differences in the financial performance of those business units. Using the revenue-growth data from this study and the standard deviations across business units, we applied utility analysis (Schmidt et al., 1979; Schmidt & Rauschenberger, 1986) to estimate the gain per business unit in moving across levels of the HS distribution. Using meta-analytic effect sizes presented in this report, and using HS1 as a reference group, the relative performance of each level is as follows:

TABLE 30

Financial Performance Gain for Different Levels of HumanSigma

HS level	Relative financial performance
1	1
2	1.8
3	2.5
4	3.8
5	4.5
6	5.2

Source: Gallup

Clearly, business units with three to five times the revenue growth of their peers are of substantial practical value to their respective organizations and worthy of emulation by their peers.

Conclusions

There is a ceiling on the utility that can be obtained by improving only one of the two engagement constructs (EE or CE). Business units with high employee engagement will not always have high levels of customer engagement. For instance, management of a business unit may create high employee engagement — setting clear expectations, involvement and enthusiasm — but the direction of that energy may be focused on something other than the customer. As well, management of a business unit may create high customer engagement, despite the engagement level of its employees — through products, location and brand. However, the sustainability of customer engagement will be at risk if employees remain disengaged across time.

The findings from this study indicate management that has focused on engaging both employees and customers will maximize its financial return, in terms of the human aspects it can directly influence.

Appendix References

Abelson, R. P. (1985). A variance explanation paradox: When a little is a lot. *Psychological Bulletin, 97*(1), 129-133.

Agrawal, S. & Harter, J. K. (2010). The cascade effect of employee engagement: A longitudinal study. Gallup technical report. Omaha, NE.

Bangert-Drowns, R. L. (1986). Review of developments in meta-analytic method. *Psychological Bulletin, 99*(3), 388-399.

Carver, R. P. (1975). The Coleman Report: Using inappropriately designed achievement tests. *American Educational Research Journal, 12*(1), 77-86.

Cohen, J. (1988). *Statistical power analysis for the behavioral sciences.* New York, NY: Routledge Academic.

Cohen, J., Cohen, P., West, S. G., & Aiken, L. S. (2003). *Applied multiple regression/correlation analysis for the behavioral sciences (3rd ed.).* Mahwah, NJ: Lawrence Erlbaum Associates.

Fleming, J. H., & Asplund, J. (2007) *Human Sigma: Managing the employee-customer encounter.* New York: Gallup Press.

Grissom, R. J. (1994). Probability of the superior outcome of one treatment over another. *Journal of Applied Psychology, 79*(2), 314-316.

Harter, J. K. (2003). Test-retest reliability of Gallup selection assessments. Gallup Technical Report. Omaha, NE.

Harter, J. K., Hayes, T. L., & Schmidt, F. L. (2004, January). Meta-analytic predictive validity of Gallup Selection Research Instruments (SRI). Omaha, NE: Gallup, Inc.

Harter, J. K., Schmidt, F. L., Agrawal, S., Blue, A., Plowman, S. K., Josh, P., & Asplund, J. (2020). *The relationship between engagement at work and organizational outcomes: 2020 Q$^{12\circledR}$ meta-analysis: 10th edition.* Gallup, Inc.

Harter, J. K., Schmidt, F. L., Agrawal, S., Plowman, S. K., & Blue, A. T. (2016). *The relationship between engagement at work and organizational outcomes: 2016 Q$^{12\circledR}$ meta-analysis: Ninth edition.* Omaha, NE. Gallup.

Harter, J. K., Schmidt, F. L., Asplund, J. W., Killham, E. A., & Agrawal, S. (2010). Causal impact of employee work perceptions on the bottom line of organizations. *Perspectives on Psychological Science, 5*(4), 378-389.

Harter, J. K., Schmidt, F. L., & Hayes, T. L. (2002). Business-unit-level relationship between employee satisfaction, employee engagement, and business outcomes: a meta-analysis. *Journal of Applied Psychology, 87*(2), 268-279.

Harter, J. K., Schmidt, F. L., & Killham, E. A. (2003). Employee engagement, satisfaction, and business-unit level outcomes: a meta-analysis. Gallup technical report. Omaha, NE.

Hodges, T. D., & Asplund, J. (2009). Strengths development in the workplace. In P. A. Linley, S. Harrington, & N. Page (Eds.), *The Oxford handbook of positive psychology and work* (pp. 213-220). New York: Oxford University Press.

Hunter, J. E., & Schmidt, F. L. (1990). Dichotomization of continuous variables: The implications for meta-analysis. *Journal of Applied Psychology, 75*(3), 334.

Hunter, J. E., & Schmidt, F. L. (2004). *Methods of meta-analysis: Correcting error and bias in research findings (2nd ed.).* Newbury Park, CA: Sage.

Hunter, J. E., Schmidt, F. L., & Judiesch, M. K. (1990). Individual differences in output variability as a function of job complexity. *Journal of Applied Psychology, 75*, 28-42.

Hunter, J. E., Schmidt, F. L., & Le, H. A. (2006). Implications of direct and indirect range restriction for meta-analysis methods and findings. *Journal of Applied Psychology, 91*(3), 594-612.

Lipsey, M. W. (1990). *Design sensitivity: Statistical power for experimental research.* Newbury Park, CA: Sage.

Lipsey, M. W., & Wilson, D. B. (1993). The efficacy of psychological, educational, and behavioral treatment: Confirmation from meta-analysis. *American Psychologist, 48*(12), 1181-1209.

McDaniel, M. A., Whetzel, D., Schmidt, F. L., & Maurer, S. (1994). The validity of employment interviews: A comprehensive review and meta-analysis. *Journal of Applied Psychology, 79,* 599-616.

Ones, D. S., Viswesvaran, C., Schmidt, F. L. (1993). Comprehensive meta-analysis of integrity test validities: Findings and implications for personnel selection and theories of job performance. *Journal of Applied Psychology Monograph, 78,* 677-703.

Pribyl, C. B., Nose, I., Taira, M., Fleming, J., Sakamoto, M., Gonzales, G., Coffman, C., Harter, J., & Asplund, J. (2004, October). Neuroanatomy of "brand addiction": An fMRI study. Poster presentation at the annual Society for Neuroscience meeting. San Diego, CA.

Rosenthal, R., & Rubin, D. B. (1982). A simple, general purpose display of magnitude of experimental effect. *Journal of Educational Psychology, 74*(2), 166-169.

Sackett, P. R., Zhang, C., Berry, C. M., & Lievens, F. (2022). Revisiting meta-analytic estimates of validity in personnel selection: Addressing systematic overcorrection for restriction of range. *Journal of Applied Psychology, 107*(11), 2040-2068.

Schmidt, F. L. (1992). What do data really mean? Research findings, meta-analysis, and cumulative knowledge in psychology. *American Psychologist, 47*(10), 1173-1181.

Schmidt, F. L., & Hunter, J. E. (1996). Measurement error in psychological research: Lessons from 26 research scenarios. *Psychological Methods, 1*(2), 199-223.

Schmidt, F. L., & Hunter, J. E. (2015). *Methods of meta-analysis: Correcting error and bias in research findings (3rd ed.).* Thousand Oaks, CA: Sage.

Schmidt, F. L., Hunter, J. E., McKenzie, R. C., & Muldrow, T. W. (1979). Impact of valid selection procedures on work-force productivity. *Journal of Applied Psychology, 64*(6), 609-626.

Schmidt, F. L., Hunter, J. E., Pearlman, K., Hirsh, H. R., Sackett, P. R., Schmitt, N., Tenopyr, M. L., Kehoe, J., & Zedeck, S. (1985). Forty questions about validity generalization and meta-analysis: Commentary on forty questions about validity generalization and meta-analysis. *Personnel Psychology, 38*(4), 697-798.

Schmidt, F. L., & Le, H. A. (2004). Software for the Hunter-Schmidt meta-analysis methods. Iowa City, IA: Tippie College of Business, University of Iowa.

Schmidt, F. L., Oh, I. S., & Shaffer, J. A. (2016). The validity and utility of selection methods in personnel psychology: Practical and theoretical implications of 100 years. *Fox School of Business Research Paper*, 1-74.

Schmidt, F. L., & Rader, M. (1999). Exploring the boundary conditions for interview validity: Meta-analytic validity findings for a new interview type. *Personnel Psychology, 52*(2), 445-464.

Schmidt, F. L., & Rauschenberger, J. (1986, April). *Utility analysis for practitioners.* Paper presented at the First Annual Conference of The Society for Industrial and Organizational Psychology, Chicago, IL.

Sechrest, L., & Yeaton, W. H. (1982). Magnitudes of experimental effects in social science research. *Evaluation Review, 6*(5), 579-600.

Visweswaran, C., Ones, D. S., & Schmidt, F. L. (1996). A comparative analysis of the reliability of job performance ratings. *Journal of Applied Psychology, 81*, 557-560.

Yang, Y., Streur, J. H., Harter, J. K., & Agrawal, S. (2020). Gallup meta-analytic study of managerial hiring and developmental profiles. Omaha, NE: Gallup, Inc.

REFERENCES

PART 1: WHAT WORK AND LIFE DO PEOPLE WANT?

Chapter 1: The Awakening

American Customer Satisfaction Index (ACSI). *National Economic Indicator: U.S. Overall Customer Satisfaction.* (n.d.). American Customer Satisfaction Index. https://www.theacsi.org/the-acsi-difference/us-overall-customder-satisfaction/

Bellis, M. (2021, August 27). *History of American agriculture: American agriculture 1776-1990.* ThoughtCo. https://www.thoughtco.com/history-of-american-agriculture-farm-machinery-4074385

Clifton, J., & Holliday, C. (2022, August 3). *The old workplace is gone. What's a board to do?* Gallup. https://www.gallup.com/workplace/395627/old-workplace-gone-board.aspx

Gallup. (n.d.). *A guide to hybrid working and managing remote teams.* Gallup. https://www.gallup.com/workplace/316313/understanding-and-managing-remote-workers.aspx

Gallup. (2020). *State of the American workplace report.* Gallup. https://www.gallup.com/workplace/285818/state-american-workplace-report.aspx

Gross, D. (2016, August 2). U.S. farms still feed the world, but farm jobs dwindle. *Strategy+business.* https://www.strategy-business.com/blog/US-Farms-Still-Feed-the-World-But-Farm-Jobs-Dwindle

Harter, J. (2022, December 8). *Splitters and blenders: Two different relationships with work.* Gallup. https://www.gallup.com/workplace/405392/splitters-blenders-two-different-relationships-work.aspx

James, C. (2018, February 26). 10 differences between French and American work cultures. *Am I French Yet?* https://www.frenchyet.com/work-culture-differences-france-america/

Kassel, K., & Martin, A. (2023, January 26). *Ag and food sectors and the economy*. Economic Research Service: U.S. Department of Agriculture. https://www.ers.usda.gov/data-products/ag-and-food-statistics-charting-the-essentials/ag-and-food-sectors-and-the-economy/

Lepley, S. (2019, December 20). *9 mind-blowing facts about the US farming industry*. Insider. https://markets.businessinsider.com/news/stocks/farming-industry-facts-us-2019-5-1028242678#while-there-are-more-than-2-million-farms-across-the-us-farmers-and-ranchers-make-up-just-13-of-the-labor-force-2

Nichols, C. (2021, June 8). Fact-check: Have one-third of US small businesses closed during pandemic? *Austin American-Statesman*. https://www.statesman.com/story/news/politics/politifact/2021/06/08/kamala-harris-small-business-closures-covid-fact-check/7602531002/

Chapter 2: The New Freedom

Clifton, J., & Wigert, B. (2021, December 7). *Bet on it: 37% of desks will be empty*. Gallup. https://www.gallup.com/workplace/357779/bet-desks-empty.aspx

Gallup. (n.d.). *A guide to hybrid working and managing remote teams*. Gallup. https://www.gallup.com/workplace/316313/understanding-and-managing-remote-workers.aspx

Harter, J. (2022, December 8). *Splitters and blenders: Two different relationships with work*. Gallup. https://www.gallup.com/workplace/405392/splitters-blenders-two-different-relationships-work.aspx

Kahneman, D. (2015). *Thinking, fast and slow*. Farrar, Straus and Giroux.

Wigert, B., & Agrawal, S. (2022, August 31). *Returning to the office: The current, preferred and future state of remote work*. Gallup. https://www.gallup.com/workplace/397751/returning-office-current-preferred-future-state-remote-work.aspx

Chapter 3: The Business Problem

Deming, W. E. (2000). *The new economics for industry, government, education.* The MIT Press.

Jones, T. C. (2020, October 19). *Retail sales by kind of business - September 2020.* Stewart. https://www.stewart.com/en/insights/2020/10/19/retail-sales-by-kind-of-business-september-2020.html

Marchant, J. (2016, May 3). *"If you can't measure it, you can't manage it"—true?* emotional intelligence at work. http://www.emotionalintelligenceatwork.com/if-you-cant-measure-it-you-cant-manage-it-true/

Chapter 4: The Role Human Nature Plays in Business Outcomes

Drucker Institute. (2011, April 22). *The fab five.* Drucker Institute. https://www.drucker.institute/thedx/the-fab-five/

Drucker, P. F. (1967). *The effective executive: The definitive guide to getting the right things done.* HarperCollins Publishers.

Chapter 5: The Most Important Habit of a Great Manager

Clifton, J., & Harter, J. (2019). *It's the manager.* Gallup Press.

Hickman, A. (2020, January 29). *What 'meaningful feedback' means to millennials.* Gallup. https://www.gallup.com/workplace/284081/meaningful-feedback-means-millennials.aspx

Hickman, A., & Wigert, B. (2020, June 15). *Lead your remote team away from burnout, not toward it.* Gallup. https://www.gallup.com/workplace/312683/lead-remote-team-away-burnout-not-toward.aspx

McLain, D., & Nelson, B. (2022, January 1). *How fast feedback fuels performance.* Gallup. https://www.gallup.com/workplace/357764/fast-feedback-fuels-performance.aspx

Nink, M., & Robison, J. (2022, June 16). *Give feedback like a coach.*
Gallup. https://www.gallup.com/workplace/393719/give-feedback-
coach.aspx

Witters, D., & Agrawal, S. (2022, December 13). *The economic cost
of poor employee mental health.* Gallup. https://www.gallup.com/
workplace/404174/economic-cost-poor-employee-mental-health.aspx

PART 2: FUTURE CULTURE

Chapter 6: The Shift

Battistelli, A., Montani, F., & Odoardi, C. (2013). The impact of feedback from job and task autonomy in the relationship between dispositional resistance to change and innovative work behaviour. *European Journal of Work and Organizational Psychology, 22*(1), 26-41. https://doi.org/10.1080/1359432X.2011.616653

The Decision Lab. (n.d.). *Why do we value items more if they belong to us?* The Decision Lab. https://thedecisionlab.com/biases/endowment-effect

Friedrich, M. (2021, March 18). *Census Bureau estimates show average one-way travel time to work rises to all-time high.* U.S. Census Bureau. https://www.census.gov/newsroom/press-releases/2021/one-way-travel-time-to-work-rises.html

Gallup. (2017). *State of the American workplace report.* Gallup. https://www.gallup.com/workplace/238085/state-american-workplace-report-2017.aspx

Gallup. (2020). *State of the American workplace report.* Gallup. https://www.gallup.com/workplace/285818/state-american-workplace-report.aspx

Gandhi, V., & Robison, J. (2021, July 22). *The "Great Resignation" is really the "Great Discontent."* Gallup. https://www.gallup.com/workplace/351545/great-resignation-really-great-discontent.aspx

Kahneman, D. (2015). *Thinking, fast and slow.* Farrar, Straus and Giroux.

Kahneman, D., Knetsch, J. L., & Thaler, R. H. (1991). Anomalies: The endowment effect, loss aversion, and status quo bias. *Journal of Economic Perspectives, 5*(1), 193-206.

Morewedge, C. K., & Giblin, C. E. (2015). Explanations of the endowment effect: An integrative review. *Trends in Cognitive Sciences, 19*(6), 339-348. https://doi.org/10.1016/j.tics.2015.04.004

Reiter-Palmon, R., Wigert, B., & de Vreede, T. (2012). Team creativity and innovation: The effect of group composition, social processes, and cognition. In *Handbook of Organizational Creativity* (pp. 295-326). Academic Press. https://doi.org/10.1016/B978-0-12-374714-3.00013-6

Sia, S. K., & Appu, A. V. (2015). Work autonomy and workplace creativity: Moderating role of task complexity. *Global Business Review, 16*(5), 772-784. https://doi.org/10.1177/0972150915591435

Wigert, B. (2022, March 15). *The future of hybrid work: 5 key questions answered with data.* Gallup. https://www.gallup.com/workplace/390632/future-hybrid-work-key-questions-answered-data.aspx

Zhou, J. (1998). Feedback valence, feedback style, task autonomy, and achievement orientation: Interactive effects on creative performance. *Journal of Applied Psychology, 83*(2), 261-276. https://doi.org/10.1037/0021-9010.83.2.261

Chapter 7: Why the Commute?

Christensen, P. H., & Pedersen, T. (2018). The dual influences of proximity on knowledge sharing. *Journal of Knowledge Management, 22*(8), 1782-1802. https://doi.org/10.1108/JKM-03-2018-0211

Christian, T. J. (2012). Trade-offs between commuting time and health-related activities. *Journal of Urban Health: Bulletin of the New York Academy of Medicine, 89*(5), 746-757. https://doi.org/10.1007/s11524-012-9678-6

Clark, B., Chatterjee, K., Martin, A., & Davis, A. (2020). How commuting affects subjective wellbeing. *Transportation, 47*(6), 2777-2805. https://doi.org/10.1007/s11116-019-09983-9

Crabtree, S. (2010, August 13). *Well-being lower among workers with long commutes.* Gallup. https://news.gallup.com/poll/142142/Wellbeing-Lower-Among-Workers-Long-Commutes.aspx

Friedrich, M. (2021, March 18). *Census Bureau estimates show average one-way travel time to work rises to all-time high.* U.S. Census Bureau. https://www.census.gov/newsroom/press-releases/2021/one-way-travel-time-to-work-rises.html

Harter, J., & Blacksmith, N. (2012, February 7). *Engaged workers immune to stress from long commutes*. Gallup. https://news.gallup.com/poll/152501/Engaged-Workers-Immune-Stress-Long-Commutes.aspx

Harter, J. K., & Agrawal, S. A. (2011). *Social time: With and whom we spend it, what we do, and its impact on mood*. Gallup.

Lyons, G., & Chatterjee, K. (2008). A human perspective on the daily commute: Costs, benefits and trade-offs. *Transport Reviews, 28*(2), 181-198. https://doi.org/10.1080/01441640701559484

Maier, S. F., & Seligman, M. E. (1976). Learned helplessness: Theory and evidence. *Journal of Experimental Psychology: General, 105*(1), 3-46. https://doi.org/10.1037/0096-3445.105.1.3

Reynolds, B. W., & Bibby, A. (n.d.). *The complete history of working from home*. FlexJobs. https://www.flexjobs.com/blog/post/complete-history-of-working-from-home/

Uy, M. (2021, March 10). *Differences between telecommuting and telework*. Lifewire. https://www.lifewire.com/difference-between-telecommuting-and-telework-2378090

Workhome Project. (n.d.). *A brief history of the workhome*. Workhome Project, Sir John Cass Faculty of Art, Architecture and Design. http://www.theworkhome.com/history-workhome/

Chapter 8: Is In-Person Time That Valuable?

Bailenson, J. N. (2021). Nonverbal overload: A theoretical argument for the causes of Zoom fatigue. *Technology, Mind, and Behavior, 2*(1). https://doi.org/10.1037/tmb0000030

Caruso, T. J., Armstrong-Carter, E., Rama, A., Neiman, N., Taylor, K., Madill, M., Lawrence, K., Hemphill, S. F., Guo, N., & Domingue, B. W. (2022). The physiologic and emotional effects of 360-degree video simulation on head-mounted display versus in-person simulation: A noninferiority, randomized controlled trial. *Simulation in Healthcare: Journal of the Society for Simulation in Healthcare, 17*(1). https://doi.org/10.1097/SIH.0000000000000587

Clifton, J. (2022). *Blind spot: The global rise of unhappiness and how leaders missed it*. Gallup Press.

Dunbar, R. (1998). *Grooming, gossip, and the evolution of language.* Harvard University Press.

Fauville, G., Luo, M., Queiroz, A. C. M., Bailenson, J. N., & Hancock, J. (2021). Zoom exhaustion & fatigue scale. *Computers in Human Behavior Reports, 4.*

Harter, J. K., & Agrawal, S. A. (2011). *Social time: With and whom we spend it, what we do, and its impact on mood.* Gallup.

Harter, J. K., Schmidt, F. L., Agrawal, S., Blue, A., Plowman, S., Josh, P., & Asplund, J. (2020). *The relationship between engagement at work and organizational outcomes: 2020 Q$^{12®}$ Meta-Analysis (10th edition).* Gallup.

Hugo, K. (2017, March 10). *Why did humans evolve big brains? We don't know, but math can help.* PBS News Hour. https://www.pbs.org/newshour/science/humans-evolve-big-brains-dont-know-math-can-help

Maslin, M. (2017, June 19). *Bigger brains may have evolved in humans because smarter people have more friends.* Insider. https://www.businessinsider.com/humans-bigger-brains-smart-people-more-friends-2017-6

Maslin, M. (2017, July 26). *Our large brains evolved thanks to an ancient 'arms race' for resources and mates.* The Conversation. https://theconversation.com/our-large-brains-evolved-thanks-to-an-ancient-arms-race-for-resources-and-mates-79183

Morris, B. (2020, May 27). Why does Zoom exhaust you? Science has an answer. *The Wall Street Journal.* https://www.wsj.com/articles/why-does-zoom-exhaust-you-science-has-an-answer-11590600269

Sherman, L. E., Michikyan, M., & Greenfield, P. M. (2013). The effects of text, audio, video, and in-person communication on bonding between friends. *Cyberpsychology: Journal of Psychosocial Research on Cyberspace, 7*(2). Article 3. https://doi.org/10.5817/CP2013-2-3

Yang, L., Holtz, D., Jaffe, S., Suri, S., Sinha, S., Weston, J., Joyce, C., Shah, N., Sherman, K., Hecht, B., & Teevan, J. (2022). The effects of remote work on collaboration among information workers. *Nature Human Behaviour, 6*(1), 43-54.

Chapter 10: Splitters and Blenders: Two Different Relationships to Work

Harter, J. (2022, December 8). *Splitters and blenders: Two different relationships with work.* Gallup. https://www.gallup.com/workplace/405392/splitters-blenders-two-different-relationships-work.aspx

Chapter 11: The Other Half — On-site Workers

Lund, S., Madgavkar, A., Manyika, J. & Smit, S. (2020, November 23). *What's next for remote work: An analysis of 2,000 tasks, 800 jobs, and nine countries.* McKinsey Global Institute. https://www.mckinsey.com/featured-insights/future-of-work/whats-next-for-remote-work-an-analysis-of-2000-tasks-800-jobs-and-nine-countries

McCarthy, J. (2014, December 30). *Taking regular vacations may help boost Americans' well-being.* Gallup. https://news.gallup.com/poll/180335/taking-regular-vacations-may-help-boost-americans.aspx

Robison, J. (2012, December 18). *For employee well-being, engagement trumps time off.* Gallup. https://news.gallup.com/businessjournal/159374/employee-wellbeing-engagement-trumps-time-off.aspx

Chapter 12: Is the Four-Day Workweek a Good Idea?

Bateman, K. (2022, January 31). *New study shows 4-day working week to be a success.* World Economic Forum. https://www.weforum.org/agenda/2022/01/four-day-week-work-life-balance-trial/

Chappell, B. (2019, November 4). *4-day workweek boosted workers' productivity by 40%, Microsoft Japan says.* NPR. https://www.npr.org/2019/11/04/776163853/microsoft-japan-says-4-day-workweek-boosted-workers-productivity-by-40

Chartered Institute of Personnel and Development. (2022, October 7). *The four-day week: Scottish employer perspectives.* CIPD. https://www.cipd.co.uk/knowledge/fundamentals/relations/flexible-working/four-day-week-scotland#gref

Clifton, J. & Harter, J. (2021). *Wellbeing at work.* Gallup Press.

Four-day week "an overwhelming success" in Iceland. (2021, July 6). BBC News. https://www.bbc.com/news/business-57724779

Harter, J., & Pendell, R. (2021, September 9). *Is the 4 day work week a good idea?* Gallup. https://www.gallup.com/workplace/354596/4-day-work-week-good-idea.aspx

Harter, J. K., & Arora, R. (2009). The impact of time spent working and job fit on well-being around the world. In E. Diener, D. Kahneman, & J. Helliwell. (Eds.), *International Differences in Well-Being* (pp. 389-426). Oxford, UK: Oxford University Press.

History.com Editors. (2023, February 23). *Ford factory workers get 40-hour week.* A&E Television Networks. https://www.history.com/this-day-in-history/ford-factory-workers-get-40-hour-week

Joly, J, & Hurst, L. (2023, February 23). *Four-day week: Which countries have embraced it and how's it going so far?* Euronews. https://www.euronews.com/next/2023/02/23/the-four-day-week-which-countries-have-embraced-it-and-how-s-it-going-so-far

Schor, J., Fan, W., Gu, O. K. G., Frayne, D., & Burchell, B. (2023). *A global overview of the 4 day week: Incorporating new evidence from the UK.* https://www.4dayweek.com/ukpilot

Chapter 13: The Reshuffling

Brenan, M. (2022, May 25). *Feelings of job security remain high in U.S.* Gallup. https://news.gallup.com/poll/392999/feelings-job-security-remain-high.aspx

Fox, M. (2022, July 12). *Even when the "Great Resignation" wanes, the workplace changes it spurred won't, says psychologist who predicted the trend.* CNBC. https://www.cnbc.com/2022/07/12/great-resignation-workplace-changes-are-lasting-says-anthony-klotz.html

Harter, J. K., Schmidt, F. L., Agrawal, S., Plowman, S. K., & Blue, A. T. (2020). Increased business value for positive job attitudes during economic recessions: A meta-analysis and SEM analysis. *Human Performance, 33*(4), 307-330. https://doi.org/10.1080/08959285.2020.1758702

Lodewick, C. (2022, April 4). The Great Resignation could last for years, says the expert who coined the term. *Fortune.* https://fortune.com/2022/04/04/great-resignation-could-last-years-expert-says/

U.S. Bureau of Labor Statistics. (n.d.). *Databases, tables & calculators by subject.* United States Department of Labor. https://data.bls.gov/timeseries/JTS000000000000000HIR

U.S. Bureau of Labor Statistics. (n.d.). *Economic news release: Hires levels and rates by industry and region, seasonally adjusted.* United States Department of Labor. https://www.bls.gov/news.release/jolts.t02.htm

U.S. Bureau of Labor Statistics. (n.d.). *Economic news release: Quits levels and rates by industry and region, seasonally adjusted.* United States Department of Labor. https://www.bls.gov/news.release/jolts.t04.htm

U.S. Bureau of Labor Statistics. (2022, January 6). *Number of quits at all-time high in November 2021.* The Economics Daily. https://www.bls.gov/opub/ted/2022/number-of-quits-at-all-time-high-in-november-2021.htm

Chapter 14: In Decline: Employee Engagement

Gallup. (2022). *State of the global workplace: 2022 report.* Gallup. https://www.gallup.com/workplace/349484/state-of-the-global-workplace-2022-report.aspx

Harter, J. (2021, July 29). *U.S. employee engagement data hold steady in first half of 2021.* Gallup. https://www.gallup.com/workplace/352949/employee-engagement-holds-steady-first-half-2021.aspx

Harter, J. (2022, April 25). *U.S. employee engagement slump continues.* Gallup. https://www.gallup.com/workplace/391922/employee-engagement-slump-continues.aspx

Harter, J. K., Schmidt, F. L., Agrawal, S., Blue, A., Plowman, S. K., Patrick, J., & Asplund, J. (2020). *The relationship between engagement at work and organizational outcomes: 2020 Q[12] meta-analysis 10th edition.* Gallup. https://www.gallup.com/workplace/321725/gallup-q12-meta-analysis-report.aspx

Patel, A., & Plowman, S. (2022, August 17). *The increasing importance of a best friend at work.* Gallup. https://www.gallup.com/workplace/397058/increasing-importance-best-friend-work.aspx

Pendell, R. (2022, June 14). *The world's $7.8 trillion workplace problem.* Gallup. https://www.gallup.com/workplace/393497/world-trillion-workplace-problem.aspx

Chapter 15: The Risk of Not Caring About Employee Wellbeing

Harter, J. (2022, March 18). *Percent who feel employer cares about their wellbeing plummets.* Gallup. https://www.gallup.com/workplace/390776/percent-feel-employer-cares-wellbeing-plummets.aspx

Harter, J. K., Agrawal, S., Asplund, J., Maese, E., Nink, M., Plowman, S. K., Wigert, B., & Witters, D. (2021). *ESG reporting on the will of the people: Public reporting standards recommended by Gallup.* Gallup.

Chapter 16: Increasing Employee-Employer Disconnect

American Customer Satisfaction Index (ACSI). *The American Customer Satisfaction Index.* (n.d.). American Customer Satisfaction Index. https://www.theacsi.org/

Harter, J. (2022, September 6). *Is quiet quitting real?* Gallup. https://www.gallup.com/workplace/398306/quiet-quitting-real.aspx

Harter, J. (2023, January 25). *U.S. employee engagement needs a rebound in 2023.* Gallup. https://www.gallup.com/workplace/468233/employee-engagement-needs-rebound-2023.aspx

Chapter 17: How to Win in the New Environment

Gallup. (2022). *State of the global workplace: 2022 report.* Gallup. https://www.gallup.com/workplace/349484/state-of-the-global-workplace-2022-report.aspx

Harter, J. (2022, April 25). *U.S. employee engagement slump continues.* Gallup. https://www.gallup.com/workplace/391922/employee-engagement-slump-continues.aspx

Harter, J. (2022, September 6). *Is quiet quitting real?* Gallup. https://www.gallup.com/workplace/398306/quiet-quitting-real.aspx

Harter, J., Rubenstein, K., & McLain, D. (2022, March 31). *Announcing the 2022 Gallup Exceptional Workplace Award winners.* Gallup. https://www.gallup.com/workplace/391211/announcing-2022-gallup-exceptional-workplace-award-winners.aspx

O'Boyle, E., & Harter, J. (2022, September 21). *Employee engagement models: Learn from the best.* Gallup. https://www.gallup.com/workplace/390821/learn-best-employee-engagement-models.aspx

PART 3: STRENGTHS TO ROLE

Chapter 18: How Do We Know if Employees Are Productive?

Carson, C. M. (2005). A historical view of Douglas McGregor's Theory Y. *Management Decision. 43*(3). 450-460. https://doi.org/10.1108/00251740510589814

Cerasoli, C. P., Nicklin, J. M., & Ford, M. T. (2014). Intrinsic motivation and extrinsic incentives jointly predict performance: A 40-year meta-analysis. *Psychological Bulletin, 140*(4), 980-1008. https://doi.org/10.1037/a0035661

Clifton, J., & Harter, J. (2019). *It's the manager.* Gallup Press.

Deci, E. L., Koestner, R., & Ryan, R. M. (1999). A meta-analytic review of experiments examining the effects of extrinsic rewards on intrinsic motivation. *Psychological Bulletin, 125*(6), 627-668. https://doi.org/10.1037/0033-2909.125.6.627

Deci, E. L., Koestner, R., & Ryan, R. M. (2001). Extrinsic rewards and intrinsic motivation in education: Reconsidered once again. *Review of Educational Research, 71*(1), 1-27. https://doi.org/10.3102/00346543071001001

Gallup and Workhuman. (2022). *Amplifying wellbeing at work and beyond through the power of recognition.* Gallup and Workhuman. https://www.gallup.com/analytics/392540/unleashing-recognition-at-work.aspx

Harter, J. (2020, May 20). *Is your culture resilient enough to survive coronavirus?* Gallup. https://www.gallup.com/workplace/311270/culture-resilient-enough-survive-coronavirus.aspx

Harter, J. K., Schmidt, F. L., Agrawal, S., Plowman, S. K., & Blue, A. T. (2020). Increased business value for positive job attitudes during economic recessions: A meta-analysis and SEM analysis. *Human Performance, 33*(4), 307-330. https://doi.org/10.1080/08959285.2020.1758702

Lepper, M. R., Henderlong, J., & Gingras, I. (1999). Understanding the effects of extrinsic rewards on intrinsic motivation—Uses and abuses of meta-analysis: Comment on Deci, Koestner, and Ryan (1999). *Psychological Bulletin, 125*(6), 669-676. https://doi.org/10.1037/0033-2909.125.6.669

Maslow, A. H., Stephens, D. C., & Heil, G. (1998). *Maslow on management.* John Wiley.

McGrath, R. (2014, July 30). Management's three eras: A brief history. *Harvard Business Review.* https://hbr.org/2014/07/managements-three-eras-a-brief-history

McGregor, D. M. (1960). *The human side of enterprise.* McGraw-Hill.

Van den Broeck, A., Howard, J. L., Van Vaerenbergh, Y., Leroy, H., & Gagné, M. (2021). Beyond intrinsic and extrinsic motivation: A meta-analysis on self-determination theory's multidimensional conceptualization of work motivation. *Organizational Psychology Review, 11*(3), 240-273. https://doi.org/10.1177/20413866211006173

Wood, S. (2018, March 22). *Where it all began: The origin of management theory.* Great Managers. https://www.greatmanagers.com.au/management-theory-origin/

Chapter 19: Systems That Work Against Human Nature

Gallup. (2016). *How millennials want to work and live.* Gallup. https://www.gallup.com/workplace/238073/millennials-work-live.aspx

Harter, J. K., & Stone, A. A. (2012). Engaging and disengaging work conditions, momentary experiences and cortisol response. *Motivation and Emotion, 36*(2), 104-113. https://doi.org/10.1007/s11031-011-9231-z

McGrath, R. (2014, July 30). Management's three eras: A brief history. *Harvard Business Review.* https://hbr.org/2014/07/managements-three-eras-a-brief-history

Rozin, P., & Royzman, E. B. (2001). Negativity bias, negativity dominance, and contagion. *Personality and Social Psychology Review, 5*(4), 296-320. https://doi.org/10.1207/S15327957PSPR0504_2

Wagner-Marsh, F. (n.d.). *Pioneers of management.* Encyclopedia of Management. https://www.referenceforbusiness.com/management/Or-Pr/Pioneers-of-Management.html

Wood, S. (2018, March 22). *Where it all began: The origin of management theory.* GreatManagers. https://www.greatmanagers.com.au/management-theory-origin/

Chapter 20: Strengths Pioneer — Peter Drucker

Drucker Institute. (n.d.). *Perspective: About Peter Drucker.* Drucker Institute. https://www.drucker.institute/perspective/about-peter-drucker/

Drucker, P. F. (1959). *Landmarks of tomorrow: A report on the new "post-modern" world.* Routledge.

Drucker, P. F. (2001). *The essential Drucker: The best of sixty years of Peter Drucker's essential writings on management.* HarperCollins.

Drucker, P. F. (2005). Managing oneself. *Harvard Business Review.* https://hbr.org/2005/01/managing-oneself

Drucker, P. F. (2006). *The practice of management.* Harper Business.

Jerkovic, D. (2022, February 20). *Knowledge workers & knowledge society...* LinkedIn. https://www.linkedin.com/pulse/knowledge-workers-society-danijela-jerkovi%C4%87/

Ricard, S. (2020, December 10). The year of the knowledge worker. *Forbes.* https://www.forbes.com/sites/forbestechcouncil/2020/12/10/the-year-of-the-knowledge-worker/?sh=6110d2b47fbb

Rodgers, R., & Hunter, J. E. (1991). Impact of management by objectives on organizational productivity. *Journal of Applied Psychology, 76*(2), 322–336. https://doi.org/10.1037/0021-9010.76.2.322

Zahra, S. A. (2003). An interview with Peter Drucker. *The Academy of Management Executive, 17*(3), 9-12. https://doi.org/10.5465/AME.2003.10954665

Chapter 21: Strengths Pioneer — Abraham Maslow

Harter, J., Agrawal, S., & Sorenson, S. (2014, December 9). *Countries with more disengaged workers less charitable.* Gallup. https://news.gallup.com/poll/179987/countries-disengaged-workers-less-charitable.aspx

Maslow, A. H. (1954). *Motivation and personality.* Harper & Row.

Maslow, A. H. (1958). A dynamic theory of human motivation. In: Stacey, C. L., & DeMartino, M., Eds., *Understanding Human Motivation,* Howard Allen, 26-47. https://doi.org/10.1037/11305-004

Maslow, A. H. (1998). *Maslow on management.* John Wiley and Sons.

Maslow, A. H. (2000). *The Maslow business reader.* John Wiley and Sons.

Chapter 22: Strengths Pioneer — Don Clifton

Asplund, J., Agrawal, A., Hodges, T., Harter, J., & Lopez, S. J. (2014). *The Clifton StrengthsFinder 2.0 technical report: Development and validation.* Gallup.

Clifton, D. O., & Harter, J. K. (2003). Investing in strengths. In K. S. Cameron, J. E. Dutton, & R. E. Quinn (Eds.), *Positive organizational scholarship: Foundations of a new discipline* (pp. 111-121). Berrett-Koehler.

Clifton, J., & Harter, J. (2019). *It's the manager.* Gallup Press.

Gallup. (n.d.). *Live your best life using your strengths.* Gallup https://www.gallup.com/cliftonstrengths/en/252137/home.aspx

Hodges, T. D. & Clifton, D. O. (2004). Strengths-based development in practice. In P. A. Linley & S. Joseph (Eds.), *Positive psychology in practice.* John Wiley and Sons.

Nebraska Human Resources Institute. (n.d.). *History of NHRRF: The Nebraska Human Resources Research Foundation.* Nebraska Human Resources Institute. https://alec.unl.edu/nhri/history-nhrrf

Piersol, R. (2015, June 1). Gallup's Clifton dies at age 79. *Lincoln Journal Star.* https://journalstar.com/gallup-s-clifton-dies-at-age-this-story-ran-in/article_cb499250-04a5-5852-b48f-282c047ff505.html

Chapter 23: Fitting Strengths to Role at the Highest Leadership Levels

Drucker, P. F. (2005). Managing oneself. *Harvard Business Review.* https://hbr.org/2005/01/managing-oneself

Chapter 25: Why Build a Strengths-Based Culture?

Asplund, J., Harter, J. K., Agrawal, M. S., & Plowman, S. K. (2015). *The relationship between strengths-based employee development and organizational outcomes 2015 strengths meta-analysis.* Gallup. https://www.gallup.com/cliftonstrengths/en/269615/strengths-meta-analysis-2015.aspx

Asplund, J. A., & Agrawal, S. (2018). *The effect of CliftonStrengths 34 feedback on employee engagement and sales: 2018 CliftonStrengths meta-analysis.* Gallup. https://www.gallup.com/cliftonstrengths/en/270350/2018-cliftonstrengths-meta-analysis-report.aspx

Harter, J., Agrawal, S., & Asplund, J. (2016). *Strengths team composition: Team strengths, engagement, and performance.* Gallup.

Harter, J. K., Schmidt, F. L., Asplund, J. W., Killham, E. A., & Agrawal, S. (2010). Causal impact of employee work perceptions on the bottom line of organizations. *Perspectives on Psychological Science, 5*(4), 378-389. https://doi.org/10.1177/1745691610374589

Chapter 26: Steps to Building a Strengths-Based Culture

Clifton, J., & Harter, J. (2019). *It's the manager.* Gallup Press.

Harter, J. (2019, June 13). *Why some leaders have their employees' trust, and some don't.* Gallup. https://www.gallup.com/workplace/258197/why-leaders-employees-trust-don.aspx

PART 4: 70% MANAGER

Chapter 27: The Manager Breakthrough

Clifton, J. & Harter, J. (2021). *Wellbeing at work*. Gallup Press.

Gallup. (2018). *Gallup's approach to culture: Building a culture that drives performance*. Gallup. https://www.gallup.com/workplace/354842/organizational-culture-paper.aspx

Harter, J. (2019, June 13). *Why some leaders have their employees' trust, and some don't*. Gallup. https://www.gallup.com/workplace/258197/why-leaders-employees-trust-don.aspx

Harter, J. (2021, November 18). *Manager burnout is only getting worse*. Gallup. https://www.gallup.com/workplace/357404/manager-burnout-getting-worse.aspx

Harter, J. (2022, September 6). *Is quiet quitting real?* Gallup. https://www.gallup.com/workplace/398306/quiet-quitting-real.aspx

Chapter 28: One Meaningful Conversation With Each Employee per Week

Bloznails, S. (2022, December 16). *18 employee recognition statistics you need to know in 2023*. Workhuman. https://www.workhuman.com/blog/employee-recognition-statistics/

Clifton, J., & Harter, J. (2019). *It's the manager*. Gallup Press.

Harter, J. (2022, September 6). *Is quiet quitting real?* Gallup. https://www.gallup.com/workplace/398306/quiet-quitting-real.aspx

Hickman, A. (2020, January 29). *What 'meaningful feedback' means to millennials*. Gallup. https://www.gallup.com/workplace/284081/meaningful-feedback-means-millennials.aspx

Hickman, A., & Wigert, B. (2020, June 15). *Lead your remote team away from burnout, not toward it*. Gallup. https://www.gallup.com/workplace/312683/lead-remote-team-away-burnout-not-toward.aspx

Nink, M., & Robison, J. (2022, June 16). *Give feedback like a coach*. Gallup. https://www.gallup.com/workplace/393719/give-feedback-coach.aspx

Patel, A., & Plowman, S. (2022, August 17). *The increasing importance of a best friend at work*. Gallup. https://www.gallup.com/workplace/397058/increasing-importance-best-friend-work.aspx

Chapter 30: The Hard Job of Managing

Asplund, J. & Agrawal, S. (2022). Boss to coach meta-analysis. Gallup technical report. Omaha, NE.

Harter, J. (2021, November 18). *Manager burnout is only getting worse*. Gallup. https://www.gallup.com/workplace/357404/manager-burnout-getting-worse.aspx

Harter, J. (2022, September 6). *Is quiet quitting real?* Gallup. https://www.gallup.com/workplace/398306/quiet-quitting-real.aspx

Why managers deserve more understanding. (2022, June 23). *The Economist*. https://www.economist.com/business/2022/06/23/why-managers-deserve-more-understanding

PART 5: GALLUP'S CEO PLAYBOOK

Clifton, J., & Harter, J. (2019). *It's the manager*. Gallup Press.

Gallup. (n.d.). *Gallup's management certification*. Gallup. https://www. gallup.com/learning/349832/manager-certification.aspx

Gallup. (n.d.). *The People and Planet 5 survey*. Gallup. https://www. gallup.com/workplace/348977/people-planet-5-survey-esg-reporting. aspx

Gallup. (2016). *How millennials want to work and live*. Gallup. https:// www.gallup.com/workplace/238073/millennials-work-live.aspx

ABOUT GALLUP

Gallup is a global analytics, advisory and learning firm that helps leaders solve their organizations' biggest problems.

Gallup knows more about the will of employees, customers, students and citizens than any other organization in the world. We offer solutions, transformations and services in many areas, including:

- Culture change
- Leadership development
- Manager development
- Strengths-based coaching and culture
- Strategies for organic growth
- "Boss-to-coach" software tools
- Attracting and recruiting star team members
- Succession planning
- Performance management system and ratings
- Refining performance metrics
- Reducing defects and safety risks
- Evaluating internal programs
- Employee engagement and experience
- Predictive hiring assessments
- Retention forecasting
- Creating agile teams
- Improving the customer experience (B2B)
- Diversity and inclusion
- Wellbeing initiatives

To learn more, please contact Gallup at https://www.gallup.com/contact.

ABOUT THE AUTHORS

Jim Clifton is Chairman of Gallup and bestselling author of *Born to Build*, *The Coming Jobs War*, *Wellbeing at Work* and the #1 *Wall Street Journal* bestseller *It's the Manager*. He is the creator of The Gallup Path, a metric-based economic model that shows the role human nature plays in business outcomes. This model is used in performance management systems in more than 500 companies worldwide. His most recent innovation, the Gallup World Poll, is designed to give the world's 7 billion citizens a voice on virtually all key global issues. Under his leadership, Gallup has expanded from a predominantly U.S.-based company to a worldwide organization with 40 offices in 30 countries and regions.

Jim Harter, Ph.D., is Chief Scientist, Workplace for Gallup. He has led more than 1,000 studies of workplace effectiveness, including the largest ongoing meta-analysis of human potential and business unit performance. The bestselling author of *12: The Elements of Great Managing*, *Wellbeing: The Five Essential Elements*, *Wellbeing at Work* and the #1 *Wall Street Journal* bestseller *It's the Manager*, Harter has also published articles in many prominent business and academic journals.

ACKNOWLEDGMENTS

Culture Shock is the product of extensive study of current and past workplace cultures and their impact on organizational outcomes. Findings were contributed by Gallup scientists, consultants and client organizations, as well as leading scientists from the academic community. While we extracted findings and condensed them into the chapters of this book, the following much larger team provided extraordinary direction, critical thinking, research and editorial guidance:

- **Editor:** Geoff Brewer
- **Gallup Press Publisher:** Seth Schuchman
- **Chief of Staff for Jim Clifton:** Christine Sheehan
- **Copy editing and writing and editing for websites and marketing:** Kelly Henry
- **Fact checking:** Trista Kunce
- **Design:** Samantha Allemang
- **Administrative support:** Carissa Christensen, Shawna Hubbard-Thomas
- **Press coordinator:** Christy Scharff
- **Communications:** Ashley Anderson, Khorshied Nusratty and Fortier Public Relations
- **Operational support:** Lisa Morock

- **Science team:** Sangeeta Agrawal, Jim Asplund, Heather Barrett, Kristin Barry, Anthony Blue, Erin Bowe-Raabe, Kristy Carlson, Michelle Chau, Carissa Christensen, Cheryl Fernandez, Katelyn Hedrick, Kate Den Houter, Sarah Elizabeth Jones, Andy Kemp, Julie Lamski, Emily Lorenz, Ellyn Maese, Emily Meyer, Marco Nink, Ed O'Boyle, Ryan Pendell, Stephanie Plowman, Anita Pugliese, Lydia Saad, Puneet Singh, Rajesh Srinivasan, Corey Tatel, Anna Truscott-Smith, Jessica White, Ben Wigert, Dan Witters.

- **Peer review:** Jim Asplund, Brian Brim, Jon Clifton, Benjamin Erikson-Farr, Vipula Gandhi, Andrew Green, Rohit Kar, Camille Lloyd, Scott Miller, Matt Mosser, Ed O'Boyle, Steve O'Brien, Ken Royal, Kristi Rubenstein, Christine Sheehan, Andy Stewart, Ben Wigert, John Wood.

We thank Frank Schmidt (1944-2021) for three decades of teaching, partnership and insights as a Gallup Senior Scientist. Frank was an inventor of modern-day meta-analytic and validity generalization methods — methodology Gallup has used to study massive sets of data across thousands of business units. The methods he taught Gallup analysts contributed greatly to hundreds of workplace discoveries that organizations all over the world are applying today and into the future.

Special thanks to the girl at United Gate F4 and RaLinda.

Gallup Press exists to educate and inform the people who govern, manage, teach and lead the world's 7 billion citizens. Each book meets Gallup's requirements of integrity, trust and independence and is based on Gallup-approved science and research.